T'

WHO THE HELL IS ALICE?

Alice Barry

WHO THE HELL IS ALICE?

JB

JOHN BLAKE

Published by John Blake Publishing Ltd,
3 Bramber Court, 2 Bramber Road,
London W14 9PB, England

www.johnblakepublishing.co.uk

www.facebook.com/Johnblakepub facebook
twitter.com/johnblakepub twitter

First published in hardback in 2013

ISBN: 978-1-78219-065-3

British Library Cataloguing-in-Publication Data:

A catalogue record for this book is available from the British Library.

Design by www.envydesign.co.uk

Printed in Great Britain by CPI Group (UK) Ltd

1 3 5 7 9 10 8 6 4 2

Papers used by John Blake Publishing are natural, recyclable
products made from wood grown in sustainable forests.
The manufacturing processes conform to the environmental
regulations of the country of origin.

Every attempt has been made to contact the relevant
copyright-holders, but some were unobtainable. We would
be grateful if the appropriate people could contact us.

For my husband, Terry

Contents

Acknowledgements

Where do I start? I didn't even know what an acknowledgement was before I began this book but my good friend and teacher Mr. Scott tells me it's my chance to thank everyone who has assisted, encouraged or inspired me to put this book together.

I owe a debt of gratitude to my wonderful friends from *Shameless*, past and present – and I mean the *whole* team: from David Threlfall, Kelly Hollis, Sally Carmen and Jack Deam, John Griffin and Lawrence Till to the producers, directors, extras, makeup and costume gang – and everyone else – but especially to the unflagging efforts of the geniuses known as the writers. This book isn't big enough to name everybody on the team but thanks for being there for me day in day out for the last nine years especially when I was at my lowest.

And thanks to the best son a mother could ever hope for, Terry and of course his beautiful wife Julie. Lots of big hugs and kisses for my grandson Shaun and his wife, Frankie, Auntie Norma and Uncle Jim and to my family all over the world. Thank to my special friend and soulmate Jeff Hewitt who persuaded and encouraged me to take this project on in the first place and to my dear friends Joe Longthorne, Barry Welles and George Lees, you aren't forgotten either.

Thanks to Ken Scott for turning me into an author. I recall discovering the joys of reading books as a small girl; never would I have believed that my book would also find its way onto the shelves of the local library. But I'm told it will be. How about that?

To all my dear friends and family in heaven, Pat Mancini and my brother Tommy and of course my wonderful parents. And to Terry, he's up there too. I know you watch over me every day my big gentle giant, thank you for 44 magical years. My protector, my rock, the best husband in the world.

CHAPTER 1

A Catholic Girl Growing up in Burnley

The year I was born, 1946, was a good year for film and television. *Great Expectations*, starring John Mills and Jean Simmons was one of the biggest grossing films of the year, as was *A Night in Casablanca* starring the Marx Brothers. Felicity Kendal and Joanna Lumley were also born in that year and some would say my destiny was already subtly being carved out from the day I reared my head in the oh-so pleasant mill town of Burnley, in the county of Lancashire.

I'm so very proud of my hometown and will defend it until the end of time. I love my roots and at one time swore I would never move away; it's a lovely place.

With my career I've travelled a lot, to London in particular as there is always promotions to be filmed people to meet and contracts to be signed, and it all seems to take place in our capital city. I like London and I like to have a little wander around the streets when I'm down in the big city – the West End shops, Covent Garden and Soho – but it's a simple fact that no one ever makes the effort to speak to you. It's a huge effort to pull the latest weather report from the girl who has just served you with your coffee in Starbucks.

In Lancashire, Burnley in particular, a stranger will speak to you at the drop of a hat and the young lady who has served your hot beverage in Rhode Island Coffee will not only present the next seven days' weather and the Irish Sea shipping forecasts but will also take time out to tell you who's been in the shop that day and who will be in later on. She'll gossip about the latest rumours and always bid you goodbye as you leave.

I did of course move from Burnley to Blackpool in 2009, helping to create the success story that is Barry's Hotel. But I swear the day I moved I left a piece of my heart in Burnley. I take comfort that Blackpool and Burnley are only 30 miles apart and I get back to my roots fairly often to take a sentimental fix of my home town.

A good Lancashire lass – that's me. I was also a good Catholic girl, or at least that's what my mother kept telling me. I have fond memories of my childhood, particularly the really young years at home before I went to school. Mam, Winifred, was a weaver at one of the big Burnley mills and Dad, Joseph, was a driver for the National Coal Board. Those were the days when you could leave your door open and not get robbed. It was a happy upbringing and there was more than enough love in the house. When I was two my brother Joe came along and aged five, just before I went to school, Mam presented another brother for me, little Tommy.

As the eldest I sometimes helped out, looking after them. Our Mam was perfect, hardworking and oozing affection. What on earth possessed her to send me to school and spoil everything? I was so proud the first day she sent me off out the door, down the road to St Mary Magdalene's School, Haslam Street in Burnley.

Mam had told me how special a Catholic school was and how I was so very lucky to have the special status the Holy Father had given me in life. It's quite ironic really because Mam was not raised a Catholic and only converted when she and my father knew that they were destined to get married. Mam had no issues with the Catholic faith and took on the new role as a Catholic mother and parent with gusto. She was 100% committed to the cause and I even remember in later life when she was on her deathbed how she begged my father to make sure that she wouldn't be buried in the Protestant section of the cemetery in Burnley. She adored my father and was paranoid that she wouldn't be laid to rest with him, with her in the Protestant bit and him in the Catholic section 500 yards away.

My parents always treated me as if I was a very special person and, well, being born a Catholic girl just reaffirmed my opinion that yes, Alice Blackledge was special. Alice Blackledge, the good Catholic girl, was put on God's wonderful earth for a purpose. Mam had a special gift for making you feel that way and as I skipped into the school-yard in my uniform I was like someone possessed, a child on a mission to learn all about life, God, the wonderful planet, and of course the Holy Bible. I wanted to learn to write and to read every book in the world. This was the first day of my life as far as I was concerned and while other little girls stood at the school gate with a little trepidation, some nervous and some even crying in their mothers' arms, I ran through into the schoolyard as if to say 'bring it on, world!'

I expected to see a few nuns present that day in the schoolyard, smiling sweetly in full battle dress with the wimple and pretty fresh unblemished faces peeking out from beneath their religious clothing; but there wasn't and I remember being rather disappointed. Nuns were certainly something to look up to and for those first few weeks I aspired to be one of them. Not to worry, I thought, they were probably inside preparing for class. This was going to be great – just what I needed to stimulate my young mind. When the bell rang I raced into school and into my first class. I recall more disappointment meeting my first teacher because she wasn't a nun either and just wore normal clothes. I didn't know at the time but there were no nuns in Mary Magdalene School. We had priests – Father Murphy and Father Corker – but they didn't teach and were just sort of there to keep you on the straight and narrow. At least that's why I think they were there.

The priests made an occasional appearance throughout that first day and I recall at lunchtime Father Corker said a prayer before and after our lunch. I thought this was great:

so many people watching over me praying for us at the drop of a hat and even the school dinners were good too. Wasn't I such a lucky girl to be born a Catholic?

Little did I know at the time but religion or rather the religion which you are brought up is merely an accident of birth. The chances are if you are born in the Shankhill in Belfast you would likely be a protestant, a remote mountain village in Afghanistan, a Muslim, and there's a fair likelihood you'll be Jewish if you happen to be born in the Neve Tzedek district of Tel Aviv. This was not something I was taught at school, however.

It wasn't long before the indoctrination into the Catholic faith started. I had looked forward to the lessons about the good book and even enjoyed the one-hour morning mass where we would sing hymns and take solemn vows. Those first few weeks as I remember them were quite inspiring and of course as a five-year-old I believed every single word that the priests pontificated from the platform in front of a huge wooden cross where poor Jesus Christ hung in torment. And he did.

I couldn't help feeling even then that surely the Catholic Church could somehow have dreamt up a more positive image of Jesus. There are plenty of stories in the Bible. What about showing Jesus rising from the dead, a huge stone behind him instead of a bloodied cross? Or perhaps Jesus standing holding two fishes in one hand and a basket of bread in the other? I always felt that someone somewhere, *somehow*, could have used a little more imagination.

Nevertheless, even though as a five-year-old I was terrified of that image and couldn't bring myself to even make eye contact with our sweet Lord, I still hung on the teachers' every word and soaked up the knowledge of the good book as if my life depended on it.

After morning mass we would be taken along to our classes and we would then say a prayer before each lesson started and after each lesson finished.

And for the first time we were threatened.

I don't use that word lightly, we were *threatened* – it was as simple as that. If we didn't say our prayers, God would know. He was watching over us. I felt as if I was being stalked and I constantly gazed up at the sky or the ceiling of the classroom convinced he would make an appearance and jab a finger at me and say 'Alice Blackledge, you are not doing what you are told. Shame on you.'

Prayers, confession, mass, the Ten Commandments... suddenly they had taken on a new meaning. They weren't there to be enjoyed any more, as my mother had intended; they were to be feared and respected and strictly adhered to. Oh no, I thought, where had they gone? Where had the wonderful teachings of Jesus disappeared to? The beautiful parables of inspiration and hope...where were the songs we sang in church with smiles on our faces? They were still there, of course, but almost overnight the sweet religion I thought I knew at home became a religion based on fear and threats. We were threatened with a fate worse than death from the start of the school day until we walked out through the gates in the evening. I told myself it was part of growing up, that this was real religion, and I believed every word.

At first the only break we got from the teachers and priests was at lunch times. We went to lunch at the Lionel Street dining hall which was next to a Protestant school. The Protestant school also ate at the Lionel Street hall but in a different part of the building and when we dined we ate in the 'Catholic Canteen'. I kid you not, even the teachers and dinner ladies called it that. I don't know what the other section of the dining hall was called where the Protestants ate but I assume it had a similar title that tripped off the tongue. The point is that not only were we not allowed to mix with each other, we weren't even allowed to sit on the same seats at the same tables – as if we were able to inflict the opposite denomination with a serious contagious disease. It wouldn't have surprised me if the knives and forks and spoons were divided into Catholic and Protestant ones too.

The Protestants ate before us and as we were marched towards the Catholic Canteen, small pockets of the Protestant children stood in groups on the street corners leading up to Lionel Street. They would curse and swear hurling abuse and used foul language.

'Roman Candle' was their favourite taunt and at times it scared me, especially when we were 'fucking Roman Candles'. An occasional stone or bottle was thrown but it was quite rare and the teachers seemed to nip that in the bud fairly quickly. Winter became a nightmare when there was snow on the ground as we had to endure a barrage of snowballs on the way into the Catholic Canteen and on the way out. It seemed there was no escape from this forced segregation of small children. I couldn't help feeling at the time that the policy was fundamentally flawed and somehow wrong – I wondered why we couldn't just all eat together.

There's an old Jesuit saying which goes something like 'give me a child for seven years and I will give you the man for life.' I read this some years back and it now makes perfect sense to me. As a child you believe anything your parents and other adults tell you and – taking a cynical stance for a second or two – the best time to convince someone to adopt a certain lifestyle or follow a particular pattern in life is undoubtedly when their tiny brains are open to anything.

I recall sitting in class or in church and not for one minute did I ever think that the adult standing in front of me would tell lies. Why should he? If Father Corker had decided to tell me that the earth was flat or that fairies lived at the bottom of my garden then I would have believed him.

We had another Priest called Father Frar. Such was his place in society that he would walk into our house most weeks without even knocking on the door. That always puzzled me and yet Mam and Dad didn't seem to mind. Father Frar was originally from Northern Ireland, Belfast. He was a jolly sort of chap; he was always cracking a joke or two generally at the expense of Ian Paisley who no one in our circle of family and friends seemed to like. I'm not surprised, Paisley always seemed to come over as an aggressive bigoted man who appeared to hate anything to do with the Catholic faith.

During the late 1970s and early 80s Paisley was on television quite regularly and I remember one occasion, I think it was in the European Parliament when the then

Pope, John Paul, was invited to speak. Whatever your denomination may be, no one can deny that Pope John Paul was a pleasant gentle, man who didn't have an unkind word to say about anyone.

Yet as soon as he started to speak Ian Paisley was on his feet denouncing him as the Antichrist and condemning him while the poor Pope looked on in bewilderment. They were such contrasting personalities and I'm sure that even a few Northern Irish Protestants were ashamed of their religious leader that day.

Father Frar enjoyed his visits to the Blackledge household – the atmosphere, after all, was always pleasant and full of fun. Father Frar was one of the few Catholic priests who never forced religion down my throat during the many visits to our house, but he was a rarity. He was almost like one of my dad's best friends and they shared a cup of tea or a small whiskey several times a week.

That Jesuit saying was probably never intended for public circulation but it somehow made its way out into the open and I think about it quite often as I reminisce about my formative years.

I am now a lapsed member of the Catholic Church and yet I still say a prayer every night of my life. While I am sceptical of many aspects of church and religion I still believe in God above. I daresay the nuns and priests I came into contact with and the teachers of St Mary Magdalene's will be quite pleased about that but it's something I can't shake off. Call it fear or good teaching or even indoctrination; call it whatever you want but somewhere along the line the teaching of the

Catholic Church has worked with me and there's nothing I can do about it. It comforts me when I pray, it gives me a nice warm cosy feeling and once I've prayed last thing at night I turn into my bed at peace with the world because I've got certain things off my chest. If that's the true meaning of religion then I can live with that. But I can't live with knowing that a certain style of teaching still persists to this day. Priests are still abusing young children, physically, mentally and sexually, and it's a crying shame that certain sections of my church appear happy to brush it all under the carpet.

Why were the teachers so cruel? You tell me. It was such a strict environment – almost military in its approach to teaching young children. At times it was as if the teachers were looking for an excuse to beat someone and always in front of a crowd of other children.

I stood in line one day waiting for the command from our teacher, Miss Fort, to make our way into school for the first lesson of the day. It was a freezing January morning and I was more than happy to lose myself in my big heavy duffle coat and school scarf. The top half of my small body was positively roasting but sadly from mid-thigh down to the top of my calf-length socks I was freezing because my legs were bare.

That was the school rules even in winter: a small pleated skirt and bare legs. Being the 'natter bag' that I was, I was deep in conversation with my cousin Annie Crossley and my friend Pamela Robinson and hadn't even heard Miss Fort call the line to order. I continued talking oblivious to the fast approaching teacher. Miss Fort carried a cane with her at all times. Teachers in those days carried and caressed the cane as if it were the most important thing in their lives. The cane's purpose was as a weapon to thrash small children – girls in my case because we were always separated from the boys.

Miss Fort didn't give me a second chance. Instead she raised the cane above her head and with all the force she could muster brought it crashing down with a sweeping motion on the back of my legs just below the hem level of my skirt. The force of the blow knocked me over as my legs buckled and I fell to the icy ground as the pain kicked in.

I had never experienced such pain – it was as if someone was holding a red-hot poker to my flesh. It was made worse by the fact that my legs were numb with the cold anyway.

As I lay crying in a heap on the floor, a thick red weal appeared on both my legs and traces of blood oozed from the wound Miss Fort had inflicted. Her aim had been good. She ranted on, threatening to beat me again, and said I was a good-for-nothing who would come to nothing and how that mouth of mine was always getting me into trouble.

I was no more than seven years of age. I can still feel the pain to this day. I hope Miss Fort is proud of herself.

Perhaps Miss Fort was right; I did always seem to court a little trouble. My legs had hardly healed when I excused myself in class because I needed to go to the toilet. As I opened the cubicle door I looked up and smiled. For some reason each 'trap' (there were six cubicles that resembled greyhound traps) had a rounded beam of wood positioned and fixed to the walls of the toilets. It was a perfect swing that my classmates and I played on whenever we got the opportunity. But I wasn't thinking as I stood on the rim of the toilet facing the back wall, grabbed hold of the beam and started swinging. It was class time and I should have been making my way back to the lesson but that thought was a million miles away. This was great fun and more than a little piece of me felt I was getting a bit of my own back on those in authority. I don't think I was up there too long but all of a sudden I froze as I heard a noise behind me. The first blow registered on my knuckles as it broke my grip and I collapsed in a heap first onto the toilet cistern and then onto the floor. The beating didn't stop there. Miss Pennington had caught me red handed and stood over me grinning. Miss Pennington was old, too old to teach I thought at the time, and she had even taught Dad many years before. But that day, as she stood in the entrance of trap five, she somehow found a renewed energy as she wielded her wooden walking stick across my back, my thighs and of course my buttocks. I begged her to stop and at one point even managed to struggle to my feet and tried to protect myself. It was no good – Miss Pennington turned her attention on my shins until I had no choice but to curl up in a ball and scurry behind the toilet bowl. It worked to a degree because the cubicle was small and Miss Pennington's power was restricted. At last she stopped and propped herself against the wall, panting hard and smiling. Yes, she was *smiling*, she was bloody smiling – she had enjoyed every second of it, thrashing a small child with a stick.

'Let that be a lesson to you, you wicked child.'

She wasn't finished. She reached inside and grabbed me by

the hair as she dragged my tiny body clear, hitting me several more times for good measure.

Beads of perspiration hung from her nose as she ordered me to stand. She pushed me towards the sinks and smiled, taking on an aura of innocence. 'Now then Alice, get yourself cleaned up,' she said softly. 'After all, cleanliness is next to Godliness.'

And she left as quickly as she had appeared on the scene. She told no one nor did she report me to the headteacher. She had taken a little break from her class and inflicted a severe beating on a defenceless child much in the way another teacher would have taken a cigarette break.

I was confused by the severe punishments at St Mary Magdalene's for seemingly innocuous deeds or plain child-hood mischief. At one point I even thought we were being punished for simply having fun, as if the priests and teachers were slightly envious of our ability to smile. Another day one of the priests caught me toppling by the entrance to the boys' school. I was quite pleased at my gymnastic skills as I threw myself against the wall and stood upside-down on my hands as I held my feet against the red brick wall. The slight problem was that I was exposing part of my long navy blue knickers; knickers that came right down to my knees. They were, without a doubt, the most unglamorous things you could possibly imagine. That didn't stop the priest. And although he didn't hit me on that occasion he humiliated me for a full five minutes as both the boys and girls looked on laughing. I turned an instant shade of crimson as he hurled insults at me, shouting 'brazen hussy' and 'Jezebel'.

'But Father,' I protested, 'what have I done?'

It was the priest's turn to go red in the face, but he was red with rage, as if a nine-year-old girl should realise the heinous crime of exposing a few inches of navy blue bloomers. I asked him what a 'Jezebel' was, which infuriated him even more as I clearly hadn't studied in Bible classes.

I later found out that the ancient Queen of Israel was a murderer and a prostitute. Rather a harsh association for a small girl doing handstands against the school wall.

I had never informed my parents about my punishments up until that point. I assumed that the respected adult members of St Mary Magdalene's were quite naturally right and began to believe that I was evil to the core.

One incident, however, convinced me that these people were not the divine righteous Christians that they liked to paint themselves out to be.

Even at such a young age the children were expected to attend mass several times a week. After a dozen months the mass became boring and repetitive, and children being children we began to find better things to do. Of course you always had to be on your guard because the teachers would always question you about the last time you offered up prayers to the Blessed Virgin Mary.

We were in some sort of mathematics class when Mr Culligan approached me. He placed his hands on the wooden desk and peered over the top of his bifocals.

'Blackledge,' he said. 'Young Miss Blackledge. And what mass did you attend on Sunday?'

I was thinking on my feet. 'Errr... eleven o'clock, sir,' I said nervously.

Mr Culligan raised himself to his full height and pushed out his chest. 'Good,' he said. 'Excellent.'

He turned to the rest of the class and said in his Northern Irish accent, 'did you hear that girls? Young Miss Blackledge has been a good Catholic girl, attends mass each every Sunday so she does.'

I was beginning to feel a little pleased with myself even though I hadn't been anywhere near the church. What harm was a little fib now and again? What harm indeed.

Mr Culligan removed his glasses. 'And who was the priest at eleven o'clock mass on Sunday, young Miss Blackledge?'

Shit! I didn't think he'd come back with that. But he knew. Oh yes, the evil bastard knew I hadn't been to mass. This was just his idea of a little fun.

'Father Corker,' I bit back immediately and for a second or two I thought I'd got away with it. There were only two or three priests who took the morning mass. Unfortunately the one I'd chosen had been laid up ill in bed. The selfish bastard!

He smiled before he vented his fury on me. That smile said that he knew I'd lied but the smile that lasted no more than a few seconds also said punishment...a punishment that he was about to enjoy.

He hauled me out by the ear to the front of the class and humiliated me. He told the class that I was a liar and that I'd committed two cardinal sins. I hadn't attended mass, that was bad enough, but I'd lied about it as well. To Mr Culligan, I was almost a criminal.

He looked at his watch and told me there was just under

an hour left in class, during which I would be spending the time crawling around on my hands and knees. He backhanded me to the floor and whipped my backside with his cane.

'Keep moving until I tell you to stop,' he said.

It was quite funny for about three minutes as the whole of the class joined in but then the first splinter penetrated my knee. I gave a little yelp which didn't even turn Mr Culligan's head. I pulled the splinter from my knee; it was coated with blood and I held it up to him expecting a little sympathy. He smirked.

'And whose fault is that, Blackledge?' he asked.

'Not mine. Definitely not my fault.'

He continued with the lesson, occasionally glancing in my direction to make sure I was still on the move. The classroom floor was made from rough wooden boards and as I crawled back and forth I noticed the blood stains seeping into the floor. I begged him for mercy, well aware that I was doing some serious damage to my knees. He ignored me apart from an occasional whack on the backside with his cane. There was no reason for hitting me, none whatsoever – it was as if he was taking some sort of perverse satisfaction. After 20 minutes I could bear it no more and stood up in defiance protesting that I was bleeding. Surely that would appeal to his paternal instincts? It made no difference. He walked over to me and struck my backside hard with the cane. 'I didn't tell you to stop,' he bellowed into my right ear.

'Back on your hands and knees, girl.'

I almost fell onto the floor. My bum was numb by now and

I could feel the little flaps of torn skin on my knees. I convinced myself that it wouldn't be long before the bare bone of my kneecaps would be showing through.

Sweet relief, I thought, when after half an hour the classroom door opened and the headmaster Mr Thornbur walked in. I looked up at him through the tears and the snot running down my cheeks and almost called out for him to put me out of my torment. He looked at Mr Culligan. 'What on earth is happening here?' he asked. I almost smiled. The old bastard was in trouble now. I'd gauge the headmaster's reaction and stand up at just the right point, and the blood would be running down my shins. Mr Culligan might even get the sack.

Mr Culligan explained my two crimes.

Now it was Mr Thornbur's turn to turn red with rage. He trembled as he spoke to me.

'Missed mass and then lied to cover it up?' he said, walking over to me with a frown. 'Is that true, Alice?'

I nodded and then opened my mouth to defend myself – to tell him about the blood and splinters and the white bone that was surely visible by now.

I didn't get the chance. Mr Thornbur began to shout at the top of his voice. He faced the class as he told them all what a wicked person I was. He always smelled of drink, Mr Thornbur. He then turned to Mr Culligan and told him that my punishment was fitting for such an evil child. As he left he told Mr Culligan that he could continue with his lesson but on no account was he to show me any mercy.

My tormented thoughts drifted back to the wonderful

stories from the Bible I'd heard as a child. Forgiveness: there were hundreds of parables and tales and verses on forgiveness in the good book and Jesus was forever forgiving people no matter how bad they'd been.

'Then Peter came to Jesus and asked, "Lord, how many times shall I forgive my brother when he sins against me? Up to seven times?" Jesus answered, "I tell you, not seven times, but 77 times".'

I don't know how I managed to survive the rest of the lesson but somehow I did. When the school bell rang I collapsed onto the floor sobbing. The class and my teacher stepped over me as they made their way out of the classroom but at least it was over.

I cried for what seemed like an eternity and rolled on my back to inspect the damage. While I couldn't quite see white bone through the congealing dirt-encrusted blood I suspected it was there somewhere. Both knees were a mess and my fingertips were bleeding too. I became aware of an eerie silence. The classroom was empty. Why had none of my friends come to my assistance? And what about Mr Culligan – didn't he have an ounce of compassion?

I stumbled out of the class propping myself against the wall several times before I made it to the toilet block. My body throbbed from the waist down and I almost seemed to have gone beyond pain, feeling instead as if my legs belonged to another person. I managed to climb up onto the sinks and positioned both knees under the cold water taps. It stung and nipped for a few minutes until the numbness set in again. The bell for the next lesson sounded and I eased my legs onto the floor. As I walked out into the corridor the other girls were heading to their respective classrooms. I headed in the opposite direction as the numbness wore off and the pain kicked in again. I climbed the school wall and ran all the way back home.

Dad was horrified when I told him what had happened. Mam cleaned me up and applied two bandages to my knees. The following day Dad walked with me to school. He marched me into the headmaster's office, carefully removed my bandages and asked Mr Thornbur if my punishment was justified and could he explain why two grown men had tortured a young girl like that? Mr Thornbur was speechless. He simply couldn't defend the actions of Mr Culligan – and in fact he had endorsed it. Dad stood and leaned over the headmaster's desk. At one point I thought he was going to hit Mr Thornbur as the headmaster shook with fear.

Dad remained as cool as a cucumber as he informed Mr Thornbur I wouldn't be coming back to his evil school. Several days later Dad told me I was going to a new school, a protestant one a mile or two from where we lived. Fantastic, I thought; it couldn't be any worse than St Mary Magdalene's.

Do I have any good memories of seeing St Mary Magdalene's School? Yes, I have one. I was made to stand up in the class one day where it was announced that I was to receive a prize for good attendance. The teacher presented me with the Sacred Heart which I then had to take round all of the other classes. I was as pleased as punch and proud as can be; the school wasn't such a bad place, for those few hours at least.

Despite my transfer to the Protestant school I was still very much a practicing Catholic girl and I was back in the confession box the following day. I wondered what I was supposed to confess about and thought for a second about mentioning the Protestant school. But I decided that discretion was the better part of valour and kept my gob shut. It was a cold day I recall, and I had an overwhelming urge to take a pee. I looked at the confession box and I was next in line. Confession would have to wait as I turned and started walking in the opposite direction towards the vestry where the toilets were. I had walked no more than a few yards when Father Corker poked his head from behind the curtain of the confession box and ordered me inside. I tried to explain to him that I would only keep him a couple of minutes and pointed towards the open doorway. Father Corker wouldn't have it and wouldn't listen, convinced I was trying to wriggle out of my appointment with the confession box.

I've already mentioned that you didn't argue with a priest in those days, particularly if you were a small girl. His word was final and before I knew it I was sitting in my seat and Father Corker had drawn the curtain (my God was that old wooden seat freezing on my bare legs!) He then asked me what it was I wanted to confess.

I thought back to the previous week and the punishment I'd been given for missing mass. There was no way I was going to confess that and get punished twice; that little secret would remain just that, a secret. The church was packed every Sunday and there was no way Father Corker or whoever it was who took the mass I was supposed to attend could remember everybody at every service and because there were two or three priests the duties were split anyway. No, I was keeping tight-lipped about that.

Father Corker prompted me again, asking me for my confession as I crossed my legs and squeezed tight. 'Please Lord,' I said, muttering to myself, 'let me think of something so I can get out of here as quickly as I can'.

'Please, Father,' I said, 'I've been a good girl this week. I have nothing to confess.'

'Alice, there is always something to confess,' said Father Corker, getting more and more frustrated by the second. 'Think hard and tell me.'

I was thinking hard – I was thinking harder than I'd ever thought in my life – but when you think that hard nothing comes. And my bladder was telling me to get up and run. *Bugger the confession box, bugger the priest, just get out there and wee!* it was screaming at me. I had to run. I stood up and moved the curtains to peer outside. Oh no... the next confessor was already waiting, as was the next one and the next one after that. Even if I wanted to run I couldn't now as everyone would think I was running away from confession.

'I confess.'

'Yes, Alice?'

I couldn't pee on the seat, no way could I pee on the seat – but I couldn't hold it any longer.

'Please, Father, please forgive me.'

'Yes, Alice, the Lord will forgive you.'

I was glad about that because I had eased my backside

from the seat and positioned myself so that the steady flow of urine which I now couldn't control fell to the floor in the corner of the confession box. I peed for England like an elephant in full flow, trying to disguise the sound with a cough. Incredibly it worked and Father Corker was none the wiser and as the pain subsided I sighed with relief and told Father Corker that I had been a bad girl. I made up a story about hitting one of my friends. He asked me why and I made that bit up too and then I was out of there with my punishment, which I believe was three Hail Marys. And I got away with it – or at least no one ever mentioned it. I was terrified when I next went to mass but Father Corker didn't say anything. The puddle of pee was too big not to notice but I suspect the next lady in there slipped out quietly, as did the next confessor and the next and so on until the end of the evening. And then the priest or the cleaner would have discovered the cardinal sin. Peeing in the confession box, sheer sacrilege, a heinous crime – surely one worthy of excommunication? So now they know and I can offer nothing but apologies. By way of defence, Dear Father, I was only 11 and it was an extremely cold day!

I was also 11 years of age one Sunday morning when I awoke early. I heard Mam and Dad busying themselves getting ready to go to mass. As children we didn't have to go to the early morning session, instead we went late afternoon or early evening. I felt strange that morning, as if I was bathed in a warm sweat, and yet I wasn't hot and I wasn't cold. I recalled experiencing stomach pains the night before and wondered if I was coming down with an illness.

I don't know why but I suddenly had an urge to check my bed sheets; they were feeling really damp and surely it wasn't just sweat. The sight that greeted me was like something from a horror movie. I was lying in a pool of blood and I mean a *pool*, it was like lake bloody Ullswater stretching from my knees right up to my navel. I panicked and starting screaming almost immediately as I put two and two together. There had been a burglary in the middle of the night and I had been assaulted.

Mam burst into my bedroom with a look of terror on her face. 'What is it Alice, what is it?'

'Mam!' I yelled. 'Call the police, call the police, someone has broken in during the night and stabbed me!'

Mam's face softened. 'No, Alice, they haven't.'

'They have Mam, they have, look at all the blood – someone has stabbed me and run away!'

It had to be the only plausible explanation. Mam said everything was okay and she needed to strip the bed and get me cleaned up then we would have a little talk.

Looking at Mam's unconcerned face calmed me down and soon after we had a little chat. She told me that it was God's way of getting rid of bad blood and it would happen every month.

'Every *month*?' I said, crestfallen. 'Every bloody month I have to go through this?'

Mam smiled. 'We all have to go through it love it's just life.'

'But *every* month, Mam?'

She nodded and smiled sympathetically.

'How long for, two months, three, four?'

'About 30 years, love.'

30 years!

That was it. That was our chat; that was my sex education lesson from Mam. No mention of the word period, eggs, fallopian tubes, missionary position, clitorises, penises or blow jobs. It was the way it was back then.

CHAPTER 2

The Unexplainable Violence of Religion

I walked with Mam to my new Protestant school, Coalclough, the following week. I couldn't have been happier. I would still see my Catholic girlfriends after school and at weekends as they lived nearby, and I would be making new Protestant friends too. I couldn't wait and skipped along the roads and pavements holding my Mam's hand with a big smile on my face.

Even though I'd been well schooled (some would say indoctrinated) in the Catholic faith and way of thinking, I couldn't help feeling how hypocritical and conflicting it all was. St Mary Magdalene's had preached to me that our creator was about love and forgiveness and how he adored little children and yet the priests and teachers seemed to go against everything the Bible and the Catholic faith stood for.

I was glad to be rid of them, I didn't need them anymore and I was glad to see the back of them. I'd make new friends at school and tell Annie Crossley all about them; perhaps we could all play together after school and at the weekends.

The first thing I noticed about the school was that there were no statues of Jesus Christ on the cross or figurines of the Virgin Mary, or busts of priests and popes. The school was statue-less! What was happening?

The morning assembly was a breeze; it was over so quickly with just a quick opening and closing prayer, no real religion, no preaching the gospel to the children. I was puzzled and had an almost permanent frown on my face, and one of my new friends quizzed me on why I looked that way.

'Don't we do Bible study at this school?' I asked.

'Of course we do,' she replied, 'in Religious Instruction class every Wednesday.'

'Only once a week?' I asked.

The girl nodded. 'Just on Wednesdays.'

'Just once a week,' I whispered to myself. 'Brilliant... bloody brilliant.'

I threw myself into my new class and worshipped all of my new teachers like the heroes that I thought they were. It was such a refreshing change to have a class that concentrated 100 per cent on the subject matter. In geography, for instance, we learned about Mount Everest in Tibet and the sheer scale and height of the world's tallest mountain at 29,000 feet. We learned that Everest was given its official English name by the Royal Geographical Society who named it after Sir George Everest, and not once did the teacher go off on a tangent and say how it was created by God or that it was a gift from the father of Jesus. Nor did she say how close the huge mountain was to heaven. She just talked about the mountain and showed us pictures in books. It was fantastic; I'd missed out on education thanks to being born a good Catholic girl but now I was going to make up for it.

I took books home and joined a library and just couldn't get enough of the study I felt I had missed out on. At Catholic school our homework concentrated on the Bible and we were expected to recite certain verses word for word and read 100 pages each week. The pupils that finished the good book were praised to high heaven (no pun intended) and incredibly given the reward of starting all over again. What? The poor buggers had to read it a second time?

I found it all rather boring and a bit of a waste of time. But not the library, with its beautiful old oak bookshelves and the hundreds and hundreds of wonderful books contained within. I loved the ambience of it all, the smell of the musty books and the polished wood and the old silver-haired librarian who couldn't do enough to help you. I can't recall her name now but she kept the library in tip-top condition. There was never a book out of place and everything was easy to find and woe betide you if you ever spoke above a whisper. *Treasure Island* and *Lorna Doone* were my two favourite books and I swear I read them three or four times each. The old librarian once asked me why I was reading the same books over and over again when there were thousands of beautiful books on the shelves. And yet she understood; she had seen it a hundred times before. I was a young girl discovering her love of the written word. I thought those books were incredible and I didn't want to change them; I didn't want to pick up a book that might disappoint me so I read my favourites more times than I care to remember. The old librarian just smiled and gave me a little grin of under-standing. What was it about those two books? They were so very different but made such an impression on me. I still remember every detail to this day: *Treasure Island* was all about adventure and action and characters with names that painted the exact picture the author was trying to portray. *Lorna Doone* was altogether different, a romance set in the wonderful descriptive countryside of Devon. I lost myself in that book and within a few lines I actually felt as if I was no longer in Burnley but on the moors in the wind and the rain walking the wild rugged terrain. Richard Doddridge Blackmore awakened something in me with his novel set in the 17th century and I remember thinking even as a small girl wouldn't it be simply amazing to be able to write a book that hundreds, perhaps thousands, of people would pick up, read and enjoy? *Lorna Doone* or the Bible? There was no contest.

I remember reading a quote somewhere from some great philosopher that religion was the biggest waste of time ever invented. I'm not 100 per cent convinced by that theory but my church and my school certainly had no doubt heard that too and perhaps just for a little bit mischief seemed determined to put a little meat on the bones.

Back at school, my new friends were brilliant, always smiling and laughing, playing little practical jokes on each other and for once the teachers didn't seem to mind that we were enjoying ourselves. I made friends with two twins, Edith and Mary Graham and a girl called Hazel Hepple. The playground was an altogether happier place and everyone welcomed me with open arms. I looked forward to playtime and dinner time each day during which I would hang around with them and we'd talk or play games with skipping ropes and marbles. Protestant girls were simply fantastic, I thought to myself.

Until they found out I was a 'Roman Candle'.

'She's a bloody Roman Candle,' one of the older girls exclaimed after her friend asked me about my previous school.

'St Mary Magdalene's,' I had replied innocently. What harm was there in telling them? These girls were my new friends, one of them had even offered sweets to me an hour or two before.

'A bloody Fenian!' another cried out as they moved menacingly around me. The girls were a little older than me and without realising they had herded me into a corner of the old brick toilet block where I'd gone to relieve myself during playtime.

Immediately I became aware of just what a horrible, filthy, urine-smelling place the old outside toilet block was. I'd never noticed it before but now the stench of ammonia filled my nostrils and entered my lungs.

'You're a fucking Catholic,' one of them said as she poked me hard in the chest. I shook my head, protesting.

'No I'm not, I'm a Protestant now – I'm at a Protestant school.'

She poked me again even harder and I fell against the old ceramic sinks.

'You can't change your religion,' she announced. 'Once a Catholic, always a Catholic.'

There was real hatred in their eyes. The girls had changed. Only a few minutes ago I was their friend and now they looked upon me as their arch enemy, as something they'd just scraped off their shoe. I'd never been punched before.

The blow surprised me more than it hurt me as the biggest girl landed a glancing punch to the side of my head. As I felt a tear or two roll down my cheek the beating started. I make no apologies for calling it a 'beating' for that's what it was. It wasn't just a few slaps, they positively battered the shit out of me. They battered me not because I'd hurt them or called them names, but because I'd gone to a different school which singled me out as different to them. Even though we all respected and loved and believed in the same God, somehow we worshipped him slightly differently.

I fell to the floor and curled up in a little ball as the onslaught continued. They kicked me around the back and legs as I protected my head with my hands.

I think it was the bell for next class that saved me. I lay in silence sobbing gently for some minutes until I found the courage to look up.

They were gone.

I stood and looked in the mirror.

What a sorry state I was in. My hair was all matted and encrusted with dirt and my nose was bleeding. I could feel a swelling just below my right eye, and my back and ribs ached like they'd never ached before. I cleaned myself up and went to class a little late. The teacher didn't even notice how distressed I was or the marks to my face, scolding me for being late before allowing me to take my seat.

'100 lines, Blackledge,' she sounded. *'I must not be late for class.'*

I sobbed gently for the remainder of the day.

My mother noticed the marks around my head and face and the rip in my school blouse. I told her I'd fallen down the steps to the entrance of the school.

The next day the so-called 'friends' I'd made from my very first day at the school now shunned me; they called me names and one or two even joined in the attacks that were to become a regular feature of the school week. I was devastated – but I hasten to add that a few girls, like Edith and Mary Graham and Hazel Hepple, were not part of this group.

In an incredible irony one day I was set upon outside of school by a group of Catholic girls. They had caught up with me by the local shops and spotted my school badge. They crowded me into a back lane and slapped and kicked and punched me until a kindly old greengrocer rescued me and took me into his shop. Eventually after several minutes of name-calling they grew bored and left. That same morning I had already been attacked in the toilets at school.

Battered in the morning for being a Catholic and battered in the afternoon for being a Protestant! How crazy is that?

For many years I wondered why I was beaten because of my religion. It especially confused me at around eight years of age when I found out that Catholics and Protestants worshipped the same God, read the same good book and followed the same set of ancient rules, the Ten Commandments. Both Catholics and Protestants believed in Jesus, Mary and Joseph and went to church on Sundays. What was the difference? I thought to myself. Would some bugger please tell me?

I now know that the rift goes back to the Protestant Reformation when individuals led by Martin Luther and John Calvin objected to the corruption, doctrines and rituals of the Catholic Church back in the 16th century. In central Europe fierce battles took place and led to open warfare between Catholics and the reforming Protestants. Right across Europe, men, women and children began knocking lumps out of each other and killing each other in the name of their God… the same God actually.

In Germany it was said that up to 40 per cent of the population died as a result of these 'Holy Wars'. And as generation followed generation the hatred continued. Even when the two Churches shook hands and agreed to live in relative harmony the hatred still manifested from father to son and so on and so on.

It's almost laughable to think that nearly 600 years on there are still individuals out there who have a problem with people who worship the same God as they do – but in a slightly different way.

I blame the parents who indoctrinate their children and the teachers who, whilst not openly hostile, can't wait to have a dig at the opposition.

At St Mary Magdalene's I had been constantly told that I was as stupid as those Protestants and if I didn't work hard I would suffer a fate worse than death – that is I would be sent to the Protestant School – and all this from supposedly educated people. It defies logic, it really does. I remember being quite surprised when I first discovered that the Protestant girls on the face of it appeared quite normal and didn't have two heads, and their mothers didn't in fact eat their children and breathe fire!

The result of such indoctrination is that small children think it's perfectly acceptable to abuse and batter other small children in the name of their religion. I hope there are a lot of people hanging their heads in shame out there, though sadly they probably aren't.

I never fought back during the attacks at school, nor did I tell my teachers or my parents. I figured it wouldn't get any worse and anyway they would surely stop soon, get bored and find some other poor person to pick on.

But bullies don't stop, do they?

They certainly don't stop when you make it easy for them and by not telling the teachers, my parents or even offering a token resistance I was their ideal plaything. The cowards were in their element.

All of the attacks took place in the outside toilet block. I tried not to drink any water so that I wouldn't have a need to visit the toilets (the only ones in the school we were allowed to use). I was constantly dehydrated and suffered some splitting headaches but it worked. For a few weeks the beatings ceased as they congregated in the toilet block waiting for me to arrive. When they realised I could control my bladder for seven or eight hours they simply ventured out into the playground, located me and dragged me in there. They were cunning bitches and waited until the teachers were out of the way before they came looking for me; they beat me around the body where my clothes covered the cuts and bruises, and hit me where my hairline would cover any marks. I got an occasional bloody nose or black eye but I always lied saying I'd been hit with a ball or banged into another girl in the playground.

I was the perfect victim. The silent witness.

I wish now I'd confided in my parents but what could they have done? Yes it may have stopped the physical side of the bullying for a while and the girls might have been reprimanded or suspended for a week or two, but then they'd be back and they'd bide their time and the name calling would start, and it would only be a matter of time before the violence started up again.

I knew I had to stop it myself.

When it eventually came to a head and I at last took a hold of the situation I had a huge regret, a regret that I hadn't fought back months before. I recalled crying myself to sleep at night and questioning the reason behind their unprovoked attacks on me. Was I really as nasty and worthless as they painted me to be? It's what all victims think and no wonder so many contemplate suicide. The thought crossed my mind too.

The physical pain I felt I could cope with; it was the confusion and lack of self-respect that tore me apart.

I remember drinking a lot of orange juice that morning before I left for school. I drank greedily at the school water fountain too, almost wishing myself into that toilet block, the dungeon of my torture for longer than I could recall.

At lunch time I needed to pee. I went to the toilet block after only a few minutes. I must have caught them by surprise because only two of them followed me in. Normally there would be five or six of them. Remember bullies normally hunt in packs.

One of them was called Mary and she was slightly overweight with long greasy blonde hair and a face full of teenage acne. She called me a 'Catholic c**t' before slamming my face into the tiled wall. I bounced back off it, momentarily stunned. The two of them stood laughing as I felt a trickle of blood seep from the wound in my head.

It wasn't the blow to my head that made me lose my temper – it was that horrible, horrible word she had used, the worst word in the English language. The word that I pray they will never ask me to say on *Shameless*. I hate the 'C' word…positively loathe it.

The girl stood for a second as I faced her. Something had changed in me and she had noticed. I could tell by the look on her face.

She glanced at her friend, a little unsure of her next move. She was older than me, perhaps two years older, and a lot bigger. She was the ringleader, the girl who had been instrumental in dishing out the majority of my misery for more months than I could care to remember, and I flew at her. I took a handful of her hair and slammed the heel of my hand into her nose as it popped like a balloon. She fell backwards onto the urine-stained concrete and started screaming as she held her hand to her face and felt the blood seeping through her fingers.

I didn't stop.

I leapt on her and attacked her like a Tasmanian Devil. I was aware of her friend pulling at me trying to stop me as I rained blows down on her head and clawed at her face. I backhanded her friend in the mouth as she staggered back in shock and continued with my onslaught against the bully on the floor.

Mary made no attempt to fight back; instead she begged and pleaded with me to stop. But I couldn't. I'm ashamed to say I couldn't.

My pent-up frustration and anger had boiled over and if it hadn't been for two teachers pulling me from her I might have still been there several hours later and eventually charged with murder.

Her friend had run to fetch the teachers claiming I had attacked Mary for no reason. The two teachers froze in shock at the scene that greeted them. They pulled me off and poor Mary lay crying and whimpering on the cold concrete floor resembling a victim of the Texas Chainsaw Massacres. The jury had made their mind up.

I was guilty. *No further questions, m'lud.*

Afterwards, as they cleaned and bandaged Mary, she backed up her friend's story claiming it was an unprovoked attack and she was the innocent victim. I knew it was pointless arguing as the evidence was overwhelming and I'd even fought against the teachers when they tried to pull me from her.

The bullies had had many victories but that day I'd won the war. The school expelled me for a month such was the extent of the damage I had caused to Mary.

I caught up with her friend who'd called for the teachers some days later in the local shopping centre. She was on her own and as soon as I approached her she covered her head with her hands and apologised for everything she had put me through and begged me not to hurt her. I stood and watched as she whimpered and snivelled like the pathetic coward she was. I told her to tell her friends – her fellow bullies – that I was no longer scared of them and to stay out of my way or they would get a taste of what Mary had had.

And they did. They never bothered me again.

I know bullying is almost impossible to police and of course each case is different, but what I will say is that you haven't got to make it easy for them. I told no one for months, didn't fight back at all and it went on and on. Even if Mary had turned the tables during our fight I still would have fought with her as I had been determined to leave my mark.

I was probably just a little lucky to win that particular battle as I took her completely by surprise but nevertheless I fought back and fought hard. I recalled seeing other bullying cases at school and the victims fighting back and in every case where the victim fought back the bullying stopped overnight. Some of them lost, a couple took severe beatings but the bullying stopped because the bully, deep down, doesn't want the hassle. They don't enjoy getting punched in the face, believe me. They want victory but they want an easy victory.

Bullying is human nature; it's the law of the jungle to pick on the weak. I do think we need to be aware of bullying and applaud the school campaigns that are in force these days. However the campaigns won't stop bullying completely and there are times where the victim has to fight.

It makes me think of Kenny Rogers's song, 'The Coward of the County'. That was me. The coward of class 3C. But sometimes you have to fight to overcome something. I don't regret for one minute what I did; in fact if I'm honest I was rather pleased with myself.

CHAPTER 3

Sexual and Mental Abuse

From that moment on I rebelled at school. I had changed; my character moulded a little harder and more determined. The priests and nuns and teachers of the Catholic school and the bullies in my new school had pushed me around enough. I thank them all from the bottom of my heart as they made me the person I am today.

I am not a philosopher by any stretch of the imagination but I have a few sayings that I have picked up along the way and that I firmly believe were made or rather written for me. My favourite is 'if it's meant to be it won't pass you by'. Quite simply, what's meant to be is meant to be and everything that happens in life happens for a purpose.

Even something as savage as bullying can have a positive effect on your life. It can help make you a stronger person which will of course stand you in good stead in the future.

I'm not saying that every kid in school should get battered and kicked around, but the real world out there is tough and if something happens to you as a young adult that hardens your resolve then take something positive from it.

The saying also makes me think that everything is within your grasp and if you want something badly enough it will come to you. If you don't want it that badly then is it really that important in the first place?

The Pawn Shop played a big part in my early life, my dad sending me more days than I care to remember. It was a real fascination to me at first, a real Aladdin's cave of treasure: gold rings and silver watches, grandfather clocks, necklaces and earrings. Dad would send me on Tuesday and Wednesday, and sometimes even the Thursday when the money was running low. He had a gold ring and watch on an Albert chain which sometimes hung from his hip pocket on his waistcoat. He was so proud of the watch, I don't know where it ever came from but it was a real treasure to him and I remember his sad face as he unhooked the chain and handed it to me.

'Take this to Mr Goldstein,' he'd say, 'tell him you'll be back for it on Friday.'

Dad would always give me the same warning every time I left for the shop. He'd tell me to be careful and run all the way. 'Don't talk to anyone,' he'd shout, 'and don't lose anything or woe betide you.'

I could never understand the logic of the pawnshop as a small girl. I'd nip along to the shop quite happily whistling or skipping a step or two and breeze into the shop to see Mr

Goldstein. He was a nice man who stood behind a really tall counter with half lens gold bifocals perched on the end of his nose. He'd lean over and greet me with a big smile.

'Well hello Alice Blackledge and what have you brought for me today?'

It was a daft question because all I ever brought to him was the gold ring and watch. If I remember correctly he'd hand me three or four pounds and give me a receipt. Dad always repaid the money together with a small fee on Friday which was payday. As I got a little older I realised it was easy money for Mr Goldstein but Dad was one of the lucky ones as he was always into position to repay the money back and reclaim his goods. Where Mr Goldstein made his real money was when people failed to repay and then the valuables went into the shop window to be sold. They were sold at a fraction of their real value and Mr Goldstein pocketed the vast majority of the profit. That's why Dad was always so careful with his money. He wasn't a big drinker or a gambler (he liked an occasional pint and a bet on a Saturday afternoon) and as soon as he got paid he sent me back to the shop with his ticket. He often sang in the working men's clubs too, he was a tenor and very good by all accounts, receiving a few quid and free beer for an hour or two's spot. This money also went into the kitty that would reclaim the items he had pawned.

What I didn't realise at the time was that we were actually very poor and this was one way of putting food on the table a day or two before payday. One day a group of my friends saw me go into the shop and ridiculed me for days afterwards. They explained to me what a pawn shop was really about and overnight I became ashamed of my visits, hiding in shop doorways near to the pawn shop and waiting for the coast to clear so that nobody would see me.

I was about 11 or 12, possibly younger, when Mr Goldstein announced that he was retiring. I'd been going to the shop for at least two or three years on a regular basis and Mr Goldstein said that he had a little present for me. I was so excited. He handed me a parcel over the top of the counter and I thanked him politely. He told me it was very valuable, worth a lot of money and I had to be careful with it. 'It's real silver,' he said and I thanked him again before running all the way home. I couldn't wait to tell Mam and Dad and I felt so proud, it was as if Mr Goldstein had given me wages for my many years of service.

I handed it to dad as he started to unwrap it. I just knew it would be a watch, a bracelet, a necklace or maybe even all of those things wrapped together within an elegant jewellery box. I was sure of it. It was square and hard – I remember feeling it through the brown paper wrapping.

Imagine my disappointment when Dad peeled back the paper to reveal a silver salt and pepper cruet set. Was he kidding? All of a sudden I didn't like Mr Goldstein. What sort of present was that to give to a young girl? I didn't even like salt and pepper for God's sake.

Miss Cook was another teacher who moulded me and made me the determined, hard-nosed person that I am today. Before you start admiring her let me tell you, my dear reader, a few tales about her and how she propelled me into my first acting role.

I was a little older at this point and suffered quite badly from heavy periods. Every few months I would be really ill and Mam would give me a note excusing me from PE (Physical Education) classes.

Miss Cook was taking PE this particular day and I handed her the note that Mam had written for me. Miss Cook didn't even read it and as I protested she pushed me towards the gym changing room. I told her I didn't have a change of clothes so she looked out some old shorts and a white t-shirt that had been lying in the teacher's locker room for years. The shorts were stinking and stained with what looked like urine, and the white t-shirt was so old it was grey.

Miss Cook forced me to strip down to my knickers and change as the rest of the class laughed and she looked on .

We were brought out into the gym where Miss Cook had placed a big vaulting horse in the centre. On a normal day I would have struggled to get over it but today it would be almost impossible. My stomach was in knots with severe cramp and I felt dizzy and nauseas. I questioned the wisdom of my poor Mam even sending me to school in the first place.

Miss Cook boomed from the other side of the gym. 'Your turn Blackledge and I don't want any excuses. Get your lazy backside over that horse.'

Her voice was loud and determined. There was no way she would let me back out.

I gritted my teeth and half jogged towards the horse. As my

feet hit the springboard I bounced off the wooden structure and collapsed in a heap…deliberately.

It was my first acting role, there was no way was that old tyrant going to get me over that bloody horse.

I played dead, letting out an occasional groan now and then.

Miss Cook slapped hard at my face trying to bring me round but I played my part well. At one point she even threw a glass of cold water in my face but my eyes remained tightly shut as my arms flopped by my side.

'She's dead, Miss.' I heard someone say.

The headteacher was summoned and still I played the corpse.

This was good. I was enjoying myself; I only wished I could have seen all of the faces looking down on me. Eventually in desperation they called for my mother. I was still lying there when Mam arrived and I heard her rushing over to me.

'Why was she doing gym?' she bellowed at Miss Cook. 'I gave her a note. She's ill.'

At this point I decided it might be a good time to come round. After all I didn't want to miss the fireworks.

'Mam,' I groaned, 'is that you?' I said, as I gradually opened my eyes. Miss Cook's face was a picture as the two-faced bitch held my hand like she was the most sympathetic soul on God's earth.

I groaned again as Mam asked me about the note. I pointed to Miss Cook. 'I gave it to her but she threw it in the bin.'

Mam turned to face her. 'Is that right? She gave you my note?'

Miss Cook was lost for words as she stuttered and stumbled trying to find an excuse as to why she hadn't even opened the letter.

'When I write a note I write it for a good reason,' Mam said sternly. Miss Cook nodded then shook her head not really knowing where to look or what to do.

Mam turned towards the head teacher. 'Can't your teachers bloody well read?' The head shrugged her shoulders.

By now I was sitting up but as Mam continued to tear a strip off Miss Cook it wasn't time to leave...just yet. Mam lifted me to my feet as I continued my miraculous recovery.

'I really do question your intelligence,' she shouted at Miss Cook. 'You're not fit to be a teacher.'

The class were giggling now and Miss Cook hung her head in shame just like the children did when she admonished them in class.

It was quite the role reversal and I loved every minute of it.

I loved every minute of my new role too...acting.

Miss Cook was very polite the next day and asked me if I was feeling better. She seemed concerned, sympathetic even, but it didn't last long.

After only a few weeks Miss Cook began to take her revenge and made my life a misery, chastising and punishing me for the least little thing.

It started with the netball team. I loved playing netball and was a regular member of the squad as we played friendlies and games with other schools. If I say so myself I was quite good playing in goal attack. The netball team was selected each Wednesday afternoon. Miss Cook would ask all of the girls who played netball to line up and notify us when the next game was and who was available to play. Around 20 of us would stand with our hands in the air and she'd pick the ones who had played the best or worked the hardest during the games lessons. We all accepted that you had to get dropped occasionally but as I was dropped for two weeks, then three, then four, before I realised something was amiss. I eventually accepted I perhaps wasn't quite good enough even though I knew the back of my mind that I was. I enjoyed swimming too and within a week or two the same thing happened there. There were even fewer places on the swimming team – about a dozen I think – but sure enough a pattern began to emerge, Miss Cook totally ignoring me as I put my hand up.

Within a month or two she had stopped me doing PE altogether, claiming I looked a little white and run down each time I entered the changing rooms to get changed.

I decided to have it out with her and questioned her team selection one day when she totally ignored me. There were quite a few girls sick that week and there were only two of us left out. I followed her into the teachers' changing area, a small cubicle with a shower, a desk and a toilet and said, 'please Miss, can I have a quiet word?'

She looked at me as if I was a piece of dirt on her shoe. 'Blackledge, what is it, can't you see I'm busy?'

'Miss,' I said, 'it isn't fair you don't include me in anything these days. I used to be a regular member of the netball team and the swimming team too. It's been six weeks since I've been playing for any of them.'

She gave a little smirk as she turned to face me.

'You have not got the right to question me Blackledge. I am the teacher and you are the stinking little useless pupil. Whatever team I choose to select is my business and no one else's. It's not your business, it's not the headteacher's business and it isn't your mother's business either.'

She reaffirmed suspicions I'd been harbouring all along. She was acting out her revenge for the incident with the pommel horse when my mother had humiliated her on the spot. She didn't have the nerve or the bravery to stand up to my mother so she was taking it out on a little girl. Only at that point I didn't feel so little, the anger was welling-up inside me and I felt like I was growing taller in front of her eyes.

I had to jump up to hit her. She was at least a foot and a half higher than me but I jumped well and timed it nicely and my hand caught her high on the cheek bone. It was just a slap but it was a good one and immediately the red mark of my hand appeared on her face as if by magic. No one hit teachers in those days – it just wasn't done – but she staggered back in amazement as she fell against the desk. I had taken her by surprise. At first I thought she was going to retaliate and lay into me but she just rubbed her cheek as her mouth fell open in astonishment.

She stuttered. 'Why you little bastard, you evil child. I'll see you never set foot in this school again; you're going straight to the head teacher.'

She grabbed me by the arm. 'Now child, you're going now.'

I was in deep shit and I knew it. In for a penny in for a pound, I thought as I turned round and clouted her again.

'That's for the netball team!' I said, adding that the first one was for the swimming team. 'I think that's about us even now don't you think?'

I was in the head teacher's office in double quick time and my mother was sent for immediately. Miss Cook didn't get her wish; I was expelled for around three weeks before she had the pleasure of my company once again. But in a way she had won; I never bothered applying for any positions on the netball or swimming team again. Yet I'd made a point and stood up to her like I had with the bullies and her authority was never the same again, not with me or with my fellow gym girls. A few of the girls even refused to play on the netball and swimming team. Everyone suffered just because of one teacher. She was an absolute prize bitch. Why do these people go into teaching?

Like most children I looked forward to the school holidays but for Alice Blackledge, the rebel with a cause it was more like being released from a long term prison stretch. Yes, the summers did appear to be longer and warmer back then – most people on the wrong side of 40 will tell you so. Perhaps you just remember the good times when the sun would shine and you'd be in the park with your friends or on the beach in Blackpool and the grey rainy days are somehow squeezed into a small box deep in the recesses within your mind.

I loved the seaside back then and love it to this day. I fulfilled a lifetime's ambition some years back when Jeff

Hewitt and I purchased a hotel in Blackpool and now live there permanently – but more about 'Barry's' later.

Anyway I'm waffling... let's take you back to England's seaside towns circa 1958. They were slowly beginning to recover from the effects of World War II. The factories and mills and the small self-employed businesses that had sprung up after the end of hostilities were beginning to flourish, and gradually the average working man found a few more shillings in his pocket to enable him to take trips to the prime locations on the north-west coast of England. Blackpool, Morecambe and Southport, each one with something a little different to offer. I simply adored Blackpool and we visited the town on a regular basis. We would walk along the golden sands and the elegant Victorian promenade for miles and miles, eating candy floss and toffee apples – and no, I can't recall any rain! Dad would hand us a few pennies which we'd spend in the amusement arcades or on the donkey rides on the beach.

Uncle Tommy, my Dad's brother, lived in Morecambe for a few years and I have vague recollections of visiting him with Mam and Dad and my brothers and sisters. He appeared on the surface a pleasant enough man but even back then as a small girl I detected that the relationship between dad and his brother was a strained one.

Uncle Tommy was very cocksure of himself even to the point of arrogance. He'd stand by the fireplace in the small lounge of his neat house, laughing and joking with us while his wife, my Auntie Claire, ran after him as if he was the King of Siam.

During one summer holiday I received an invite from Uncle Tommy to spend a few days with them. I was so excited, I'd never stayed overnight anywhere else other than our home in Bread Street in Burnley and to stay in such an elegant fun-packed place as Morecambe, well that was simply the best news of the year!

Dad was a little reluctant to let me go away on my own but between Mam and I we badgered him until eventually he gave in.

I was 'Little Miss Independent' as I sat on the bus to Morecambe with my cheese sandwiches and my carton of squash, a packet of crisps and a chocolate bar. I'd finished the lot before the bus left Blackburn Road about a mile from the town centre.

After a few hours on the bus I was nearly peeing myself with excitement when I spotted the sign by the side of the road that told me the bus had officially entered the boundary limits of Morecambe. My Aunt and Uncle were there to meet me as the vehicle pulled into the station in Morecambe.

The next morning Uncle Tommy and Aunty Claire told me we would be going to the beach for the day. Just before we left my Uncle Tommy knocked on my bedroom door. He handed me a bag with something in it.

'Put this on for the beach,' he said. 'All the girls are wearing these and it will keep you cool.'

I opened the bag to reveal a thin pale green sun top. I was horrified as I'd never worn anything like that before. At that particular point in time I'd started puberty and developed quite a nice bust thank you very much! However, all my clothes were loose fitting – my dresses and blouses were rather baggy and drab. The sun top wrapped around me and fastened like a bra at the back. As I studied myself in the mirror the top clung to my breasts leaving little to the imagination and my nipples could clearly be seen. I was in a no-win situation. I didn't want to offend Uncle Tommy, but nor did I want to wear a top that exposed my breasts so much. I decided on a compromise: I left it on but pulled a t-shirt over the top to hide my modesty and made my way downstairs.

Uncle Tommy stood in his familiar stance at the fireplace but as I walked in his face fell as a look of disappointment washed over him.

'Why Alice,' he said, 'don't you like your new top? It cost Auntie Claire a fair packet.'

I felt so guilty and explained that I might consider taking my top off at the beach. As we got to the beach it was baking hot and Uncle Tommy constantly reminded me about the new sun top. He went on and on about how I would feel a lot more comfortable without my t-shirt. He pointed to the other girls on the beach and told me it was the fashion. I didn't disagree but at the same time the other girls looked so much older than me. After about half an hour I eventually decided to take my t-shirt off and just thanked God Dad wasn't there to see me. I sat for most of the day with my arms folded.

After a few hours Uncle Tommy suggested we all cooled off in the sea. It was absolutely perishing at first but after a few minutes splashing around, the water became bearable and then quite pleasant as I dived in and out the white surf. I then became aware of Uncle Tommy standing in front of me with a camera.

'Give me a smile,' he said.

I immediately went on the defensive, covering myself up. 'I'd rather not,' I told him. 'I don't think my dad would approve.'

Uncle Tommy told me not to be so stupid, as it was just a photo for the family album. I looked across at Auntie Claire who nodded her head gently, so I relented. As I walked back over to where our towels were I gazed self-consciously down at my chest. Argh...I was horrified. My rock-hard nipples were sticking out like bloody organ stops. How did I know cold water would do that to my young body? I couldn't get my t-shirt on quick enough, making the excuse that I was cold.

After a few days I took the bus home back to Burnley. Dad was waiting for me when I walked back into the lounge. He held the photograph up above his head.

'Do you want to tell me the meaning of this, young lady?' he roared at me.

For some reason Uncle Tommy, the horrible, horrible dirty bastard, had decided to send Dad the photograph.

I was speechless, ashamed; it was as if I had been in on Uncle Tommy's little ruse to upset Dad. He went mad and kept me in the house for the next two weeks.

It was some time before the two brothers spoke again and eventually Uncle Tommy moved back to Burnley. He bought a secondhand shop in Accrington Road in town and asked my dad if I would like a job on Saturdays when the shop was at its busiest.

I jumped at the chance to earn a little extra pocket money and readily agreed. Uncle Tommy told me to come along to the house one evening and he would fill me in on the details. I went along to Uncle Tommy and Aunty Claire's house quite often. I didn't have a key and always just walked in. One day I wished I hadn't. Uncle Tommy had suffered from bouts of malaria since he had returned from India and occasionally took to a bed which Auntie Claire and he had moved down from the spare bedroom to the living room. Sure enough as I breezed into the lounge unannounced Uncle Tommy was flat on his back. But there was also someone else there, kneeling on the floor with her head in his lap bobbing up and down, and as I looked on a little puzzled I realised that Uncle Tommy was naked with a contorted look on his face and he was groaning. And then she stopped, climbed up and I seemed to realise that something wasn't quite right and I slinked back into the hallway. They exchanged a few words and I heard a goodbye. Why was Auntie Claire leaving? I looked at my watch. It was nearly tea-time and it would soon be time for her to make dinner.

All of a sudden she appeared in the hallway. Only it wasn't Auntie Claire it was the next door neighbour, Mrs Jackson. She didn't say anything but ruffled my hair as she walked past me. As she reached the door she turned around looked at me and placed a finger across her lips. She was telling me to keep quiet. I didn't quite understand what she had been doing but I knew enough to realise that it wouldn't have been something Auntie Claire would have approved of.

I didn't see Uncle Tommy that night or Auntie Claire. Instead I turned tail and ran all the way back home.

And the very next week I stood outside his shop at nine o'clock sharp just as Uncle Tommy opened up. The magical treatment he had received at the hands of his pretty next-door neighbour had brought him back to full health. The shop was rather quiet and I remember being quite puzzled as to why Uncle Tommy had called on my help. On that first Saturday there couldn't have been more than a dozen people who called into the shop. Nevertheless Uncle Tommy sold a tatty old three-piece suite, two desks, a standard lamp and at least three or four other pieces of junk. He seemed more than happy with his day's work while I sat and twiddled my thumbs doing nowt! If I remember correctly I wrapped one vase in eight hours. It was easy money; not exactly a hard day's work.

The following Saturday was really quiet and Uncle Tommy decided to close the shop at lunchtime. He sent me out to the chip shop for some fish and chips and we went into the back office to eat. This was great fun I thought; money for old rope and fish and chips too!

When we had finished Uncle Tommy announced we were to play hide the thimble. He took out a thimble from his pocket and told me to close my eyes. When I opened them he stood with a smile on his face and told me to start searching him. I found the thimble in his shoe. When it was my turn I decided to hide the thimble somewhere in the office. When he started to touch and feel and search around my body I would tell him he was cold. As he searched the office I would tell him he was getting warmer and eventually hotter and hotter until he found it. Uncle Tommy always hid the thimble on his person, and more often than not he would encourage me to search for it in his front trouser pockets.

I was about twelve at the time and hadn't even seen a willy let alone touched one. As I fumbled in Uncle Tommy's pocket I touched something big and hard but couldn't work out what it was. I knew however it was much too big to be a thimble.

Uncle Tommy noticed the confusion on my face.

'You're wondering what that is aren't you?'

I shook my head; somehow I knew that anything located in his trouser region wasn't something I should be taking any notice of.

In an instant Uncle Tommy's trousers were on the floor and he stood proudly as his huge willy stuck up in the air.

'Come and touch it, Alice,' he begged. 'It will be our little secret.'

I confess I was fascinated at what was unfolding in front of me and my jaw literally hit the deck.

Picture the scene: Alice Blackledge, thick jam-jar National Health glasses, head tilted slightly forward with her mouth wide open as Uncle Tommy stood with his trousers at his feet waving his rather impressive wedding tackle.

What on earth was making it stand up in the air and why was it so big?

Uncle Tommy took a step forward. 'Come on, Alice, let me put it between your legs. It will feel so nice.'

I instinctively backed away, shaking my head. Uncle Tommy sensed my fear.

'Just touch it, Alice, just touch it for today. When you get used to it I can put it inside you.'

Inside me? Inside *where*? The man was mad!

'Do this to it, Alice.' he said. 'Just do this for today.'

At first he'd just been stroking himself, but now he was holding his willy and his hand was moving back and forth, getting quicker all the time.

I wanted out of that shop as I felt a tightness pull across my chest. Although I didn't know what Uncle Tommy was doing at the time I sensed it was wrong. Uncle Tommy grabbed for my hand as he tried to get me to touch him but I pulled away, backing into the corner of the shop. His hand was a blur now as he started moaning and telling me how good it was. I stood gobsmacked, unable to tear my eyes away from the amazing spectacle of my uncle clearly pleasuring himself.

He pulled at himself for two or three more minutes, moaning ever louder and staring at me with a look on his face that I had never seen on a man before.

Then he ejaculated.

He gave out a loud groan as what seemed like a fountain of white liquid exploded from the end of his willy. I remember thinking at the time that he had somehow broken it.

It was disgusting. It was everywhere; on his trousers, the desk and the floor and it smelled horrible.

Uncle Tommy was smiling as he pulled his trousers up.

'I'd better open the shop up,' he said calmly as he looked

at his watch. 'Don't you be going telling your Dad about this because he won't believe you.'

Uncle Tommy proceeded to tell me how his little game would progress as the weeks went on. He would teach me how good it was and where it was supposed to fit, and he would teach me how to stroke it quickly like he did. I would be so happy when he pushed it between my legs, he said, and it would always be our little secret.

I never said a word in reply as he described the act of sex and how his bits and girls' bits fitted together. He said it was a natural part of life – part of growing up.

I couldn't get out of the door quick enough. When I got home I told my dad I didn't want to go back to his brother's shop anymore. Dad never asked me why, he just said that if I didn't want to do anything I didn't have to.

I never told Dad what his brother had done; it would have broken his heart. Like most abuse victims I simply sealed my lips. They're all dead now: Dad, Mam and Uncle Tommy. But I think Dad knew what his brother was like. Tommy never cared about anyone else and Dad once told me that whilst in India with the British Army, Uncle Tommy had married an Indian girl who had washed and cooked and cleaned and served and cared for him for over three years. When Uncle Tommy was due to leave he took her out into the middle of a busy street and made her kneel down in front of him and say 'I divorce thee' three times.

In the Muslim world that is all that is necessary for a man to be granted a divorce from his legal wife. It is known as pronouncing the *talaq*, the formula of repudiation. The first two times the *talaq* is pronounced it may be withdrawn. This is designed to give the husband time to control his temper or to think things over, but saying it a third time makes the divorce irrevocable.

Uncle Tommy's wife was an outcast, thrown out of her community as soiled goods – a worthless piece of shit. Uncle Tommy walked away and thought no more about her; he was on his way home and she was an unnecessary inconvenience.

Dad often asked him if he felt even a tiny pang of guilt towards her but he simply laughed it off and treated it as a huge joke.

It saddens me to say this but that was Uncle Tommy. Looking back, I think my dad always suspected his brother was a pervert.

Somehow I wanted to detail this episode of my life in this book. I wanted to somehow get it off my chest…the experts call it 'closure'.

My abuse was minimal and of course Uncle Tommy didn't physically harm or touch me. But if I'd continued to go to his shop it would have been a green light for him to continue doing what he was doing and I've no doubt whatsoever that eventually he would have forced himself upon me.

As a small girl I truly believed he was my adoring loving uncle but he wasn't, he was a dirty bastard. I couldn't even bring myself to go to his funeral, how sad is that?

As a footnote, Uncle Tommy is buried in the same cemetery as my dad and my brother Tommy. My husband Terry is there too – quite a family collection. I visit as often as I can especially on an important anniversary or a birthday. I buy flowers from the local flower stall and spread them around on everyone's grave. That is, everyone except Uncle Tommy's. I can't bear to throw a single petal on that man's grave. I'm sure Dad would understand, he might even agree with me.

CHAPTER 4

Prison Fodder, That's Me

Miss Baldwin was another teacher who shouldn't have gone anywhere near a classroom full of children. I have two distinct memories of Miss Baldwin that are as clear to me now as when they happened over 50 years ago.

They will not go away; they are locked into my memory.

They shouldn't be.

I should have images of a smile, a kindly word here and there and memories of a poignant moment in a history lesson or a detailed description of a strange country and its people explained by a woman in her prime, a teacher in her element in a career she adored.

I haven't.

I see a bitter, twisted, middle aged woman who would rather be stuck at home knitting or watching daytime TV. It's all so very sad.

Miss Baldwin taught art and as sure as eggs are eggs I couldn't draw to save my life…not even an egg!

It was as simple as that, but *boy* did Miss Baldwin enjoy it. 'That's rubbish,' she'd yell as she stood over me. I'd want to yell 'yes! I know I can't help it.' Then she'd rap my knuckles with her heavy ruler and I'd yelp out in pain.

'Start again,' she'd announce and with my knuckles throbbing like hell I'd pick up the pencils or the paint brush and start all over again.

But one day she really annoyed me. For once my attempt in copying Van Gogh's sunflowers was at the very least half-good. There was something about the copy she'd hung on the blackboard. The colours were vibrant; they seemed to express real emotion and yet a simplistic, unreal, beauty. Some of the flowers were in full bloom, some wilting and brown. Something drew me into the painting and made me want to take my time and at least have a good go at it.

As the painting took shape my normally useless brush hand took on a mind of its own and for the first time ever in an art class I could make sense of what was beginning to form. I looked up every four or five seconds to study the image, correct where I'd went wrong and add some more paint to the work.

Miss Baldwin stood at the front of the class and read from a book as we splashed the watercolours onto the paper. 'Van Gogh first began painting sunflowers after he left Holland for France,' she said. 'The first flowers in vases were created simply to decorate his friend's bedroom.'

I looked up occasionally and dare I say it, Miss Baldwin (if you are reading this), I even took a little inspiration from you. I confess you looked a little bored but nevertheless your words sank in and are with me to this day, so you must have been doing something right.

And then she ruined the moment.

I was so wrapped up in my painting that I hadn't even noticed her begin her ritual patrol. She closed the book and began wandering amongst her flock. She stood over me with her inch-thick ruler poised as I sat with my tongue lolling out of the side of my mouth, lost in my thoughts.

She brought it crashing down on my knuckles and as I jumped up with a start she whipped the page away from me.

She turned to the class. 'This is absolute rubbish,' she announced and as I looked on in horror she tore the paper in two, then four, crumpled it up and threw it into the bin.

'No!' I cried. 'No, you horrible bitch!'

It was the best thing I had ever drawn. I can see the image to this day and I was proud of it. Miss Baldwin knew; she knew I'd given it my best and she also knew that although it may not grace a spot in a gallery it was a perfectly acceptable attempt for a young girl not possessed with an artistic flair or an eye for colour.

'You horrible nasty bitch,' I repeated.

No one had called her that name before. She lunged at me and grabbed me by the hair and marched me towards the cupboard that stored the paint pots and brushes, the easels, the crayons and other materials associated with an art class. She threw me in and closed the door. I begged her to open the door explaining that I was claustrophobic but to my horror she turned the key in the lock.

It was pitch-black and even as my eyes grew accustomed to the dark I began to panic, banging on the door ever louder.

Miss Baldwin ignored me and carried on with the lesson.

It was time to make her pay, I thought. It was time to really make her pay.

I started with the top shelf. Dozens and dozens of glass jars full of turpentine with perhaps 20 brushes in each. I threw them all onto the floor.

Paper next. Newspaper, coloured paper, wall paper and tissue paper – any paper I could find. I threw it onto the floor and mulched it into a papier-mâché mixture.

The pots of clay filled with water were next; a potter's wheel that I powered into the concrete floor as it smashed into a hundred pieces; a huge box of rulers, glass bottles and jars, and finally small tubes of acrylic paint that I stamped on until they burst wide open.

I heard Miss Baldwin on the other side of the door frantically fumbling with the key in the lock as she yelled out to me to stop. She couldn't get in. I had wedged the door shut against the far wall with the backbone of an easel.

She would get in when I was finished. Everything came off the shelves and I mean everything. The pile on the floor was getting bigger as I felt myself growing ever taller. I stamped and jumped and the mushy wet mixture flew everywhere – on the walls, on the ceiling, on the back of the door and even up my skirt. I stopped for a few seconds and could feel the paint running down my legs. I put my hands in the mixture and rubbed it in. I was ready for her. Just let her try and get hold of me – she'd end up looking like Sitting Bull on a bad day.

Eventually I let her in. What a bloody mess I stood in.

Now that's what I called 'art' – a new type of expressionism, perhaps? When the door opened I simply smiled at the fuming teacher. She couldn't believe what she was looking at and I saw it in her eyes, she realised she'd screwed up big time.

'I'm sorry Miss Baldwin,' I said, 'but I did tell you I was claustrophobic.'

I have pleasant memories from my school years, of course I have, and there were one or two teachers that even to this day I have a great love and respect for, but they were few and far between. The profession has changed somewhat and times have moved on: teachers are more in touch with the pupils and appear to be able to relate to them more. Some teachers these days are even called by their Christian names. I'm not sure I agree with that one but nevertheless it suggests a more level playing field. When I was at school we were treated like second-class citizens. We had to know our place and could only speak when we were spoken to. There was never any question of a pupil discussing the teacher's teaching methods or offering an opinion as to how to approach a subject. No; we were pupils and they were teachers and they ruled with a rod of steel.

As I said there were exceptions. Miss Pedlar took our domestic science class, a lesson I looked forward to every week. I'm not sure what the 'Politically Correct Brigade' would make of our domestic science lesson these days and needless to say it was an all-girls class. We were told to do everything you would associate with the stereotypical role of the house wife back in the 1960s: Miss Pedlar would show us how to iron, cook, sew and clean, and the class even had a small bathroom towards the rear of the room which was used to demonstrate how to bathe babies and small children.

That was all well and good but I think the education authorities slipped up somewhere because the vast majority of the girls in my class didn't even have a bath let alone a bathroom. Our houses were the typical two-up-two-down terraced affair – that is to say two bedrooms upstairs with a lounge and the kitchen on the bottom level. Bathrooms? Don't make me laugh; we had a tin bath that made its appearance on a Friday evening and whether you needed a wash or not you were scrubbed in front of the fire in full view of anyone who happened to be in the room. The bathwater was topped up from a kettle as each child took his or her turn. When Miss Pedlar first showed me the bath I was dumbfounded; I had never seen a big bath before except in a newspaper or magazine. Miss Pedlar knew who the poor children were and which of us didn't have a bathroom. She would allow us the luxury of a bath as we took turns during the lesson. There was a never-ending supply of piping hot water and the teacher would insist on a crystal clear clean bath for every girl that wanted one. I think we were allowed 15 minutes each and Miss Pedlar squeezed four or five girls into every lesson! I was in sheer heaven when eventually my name was called. I couldn't wait to get my clothes off and Miss Pedlar always had a never-ending supply of big fluffy towels stacked up on a seat by the bath. It's difficult to comprehend these days: a teacher in a classroom allowing small girls to take off their clothes and jump into a hot bath, but back then it seemed the most natural thing in the world.

Miss Pedlar taught me just about everything I knew about cooking and we were allowed to take cakes home at the end of the lesson. Over breakfast one day I happened to mention to my Mam that we would be making jam tarts in Miss Pedlar's lesson and my two little brothers whooped for joy. Cakes were a luxury back then and I mean a real luxury; apart from Miss Pedlar's class, cakes were restricted to birthdays and Christmas time or for a really special occasion. The jam tarts turned out perfect, several different colours filled with strawberry, blackcurrant and apricot jam. The strawberry one tasted so good as I walked out of the school yard with the tarts in tow. What was the harm, I thought to myself as I munched a blackcurrant one a short while after; one or two won't make any difference. The trouble with me was I talked too much and on that particular day, as I walked home with my friends, I talked and talked and talked and when I talk I lose concentration. I remember sharing one of the jam tarts with my friends and another fell on the floor; I also remember a particularly tasty apricot jam one as I passed by the bottom of our street. But imagine my sheer panic when I lifted the lid on the box as I approached our front door to find nothing in there but a few crumbs. I was mortified – no way could I have eaten all of those jam tarts!

Then my tummy started to ache and the truth dawned on me: there must've been at least 16 jam tarts in that box, enough for everyone and plenty to share around.

I felt so guilty, especially when I set eyes on my expectant brothers' faces sitting at the kitchen table. At first they thought I was hiding the jam tarts in my satchel, but eventually after several minutes they realised I wasn't play acting.

The incident with the jam tarts was never forgotten and Mam and Dad and my brothers teased me relentlessly for many a month. But I never opened the lid of the box from the cookery class again and everything I made was duly brought home completely intact. It was another of life's little lessons and something that I still look back on with a smile.

Miss Baldwin was still my teacher when I eventually left Coalclough School at the age of 15. We had a picnic on the final day where we were supposed to talk to the teachers about our aspirations and dreams for the future. It was a nice party atmosphere and for once most of the teachers treated us like adults.

I suppose, figuratively speaking, we were adults because most of the class had already secured positions at the local mills to start work. That was about as ambitious as working class Burnley was at that time; you left school and took a job at a mill that was it.

I hadn't yet gone down that route, figuring I'd have a month or two off before deciding what it was I was going to do. Towards the end of the afternoon Miss Baldwin approached me.

'Got yourself a job lined up, Blackledge?'

I shook my head. 'No Miss, not yet.'

Miss Baldwin smirked. 'I thought not Blackledge, your future is already mapped out I'm afraid.'

I wasn't sure what she meant but judging by the smile on her face it wasn't too complimentary.

'What do you mean Miss?' I asked.

She leaned forward and spoke. I can still remember the smell of her stale wicked breath.

'Prison fodder,' she whispered. 'That's you, my girl: prison fodder.'

She turned around smiling and tried to walk away but I grabbed her jacket and held her there. 'Just you watch, Miss,' I said. 'Just you watch the years go by and see what happens to me.'

I've already said that things in life are put there for a purpose. The character of Miss Baldwin was no accident to Alice Blackledge. My Guardian Angel placed Miss Baldwin into my life to give me a determination to succeed. Whenever I've felt like giving up on a dream I remember Miss Baldwin's parting shot about 'prison fodder' and even to this day she serves me well.

My schooling taught me to read and write and helped mould my character and resolve. Sadly it didn't give me much more and I left school that day feeling a little cheated. Qualifications? I don't think we had any and if there was such a thing I didn't have a certificate to present to an employer (not that they ever asked for certificates in those days). There was no such thing as 'further education' in my school back then and no one in my class went onto college or university. Children today have far more opportunity and anyone can aspire to further education or even university. That said, I think it's probably gone too far and there's an immense amount of pressure placed on kids to stay on. It's a fact that some are ready to leave at 16, some want to leave and make their way into work and business; but there's always someone ready to call them a failure. Schooling isn't everything and nor is university suited to everyone too. There will always be bricklayers and builders and bin-men and shop assistants and people needed to work in factories, and you certainly don't need any pieces of paper or certificates to be an actress. (Thank God!) It doesn't mean they've failed it's just their life choice and we can't all end up being doctors and brain surgeons.

As I walked home by the Leeds Liverpool Railway Line I threw my books and satchel over the dirty brown fence designed to keep people off the tracks.

It was a poignant moment and at that particular point in time I couldn't help feeling that the system had somehow cheated me. Although university wasn't an option I somehow felt that the system hadn't worked and given me what I was entitled to. Perhaps I had been unlucky, a little unfortunate to come into contact with teachers who couldn't be arsed.

But as I picked up my pace and walked along the street I began to feel cleansed and invigorated, as if a ton weight had been lifted from my shoulders. My school life was over and I was ready to take on the world.

When I got home I told Mam about my satchel. I thought she'd be furious but she wasn't. She smiled and wrapped her arms around me and asked me what I wanted to do with my life.

I shrugged my shoulders and told her I didn't have a bloody clue.

CHAPTER 5

Keeping My Dignity Intact

Carlos was simply gorgeous and he was making eyes at me. He was definitely the most handsome boy in town. He was tall and slim with a shock of jet black hair swept back from his face. He was a little older than me, perhaps 18 or 19 and all of the girls in town fancied him.

He took me to see *The Nun Story* at the cinema for our first date. *That's nice*, I thought. Audrey Hepburn was beautiful, Peter Finch played a brilliant role and Carlos acted like a true gentleman, not even attempting as much as a kiss on the first night. We went back to the same cinema a week later but this time the film was in French with subtitles. What a difference from *The Nun Story* – the French film was all sex and nudity, heaving sweating bodies and large breasted girls moaning and groaning with pleasure.

Carlos couldn't tear his eyes from the screen for two hours.

After the pictures he said he was taking me to a club for a drink. En route to the club he pulled me gently into some garages on the way. They were dimly lit and quiet and I remember being up for a little kiss and cuddle, something I hadn't done before but my girlfriends had told me all about. Urgh...wasn't that first wet kiss horrible? Horrible and then actually quite nice after a few seconds. Carlos pressed into me, grabbing at my backside and breathing hard while we kissed clumsily. I needed to breathe too and I pushed him away as I gasped for some air. As we parted I instinctively looked down and you can guess what he was holding in his hands.

'You can put that bloody thing away,' I roared at him as I stormed off.

He caught up with me after a few hundred yards, apologising and said he was only testing. 'I'm glad you did that Alice, it means you are a good girl.'

I fell for it. I actually bloody believed that he'd set up a little test for me and so I agreed to go to the club with him.

I remember being a little nervous as I was only 16 and 18 was the age to get in but Carlos said I looked much older and that he knew the men on the door. We got in without a problem and Carlos wanted to buy me something alcoholic but I refused. He ordered a pint of beer and stood trying to look cool propped against the bar. He didn't look cool to me; I noticed he was very fidgety and perspiring quite a lot. I asked him if he was okay but he just said the club was too hot. We left shortly afterwards and Carlos said he would walk me home. Carlos was acting really strange as we walked past Scott Park, breathing heavily and looking quite ill. I asked him again if he was okay.

Suddenly he lunged at me and dragged me into the park. I thought he was just joking at first but quickly realised he was being far too rough for a little bit of play acting. He pulled me over to some bushes and threw me to the ground, tearing at my clothes; he stood over me and fumbled with his flies before pulling out his willy (what is it with me that makes men want to get their willies out?).

I scrambled to my feet shouting at him to leave me alone but he grabbed me again and threw me back into the dirt and I realised I was in a real fight, a fight for my dignity, my virginity and, who knows, even my life.

And fight I did.

I was back in that toilet block again as shock turned to anger and then the realisation that this was serious. We fought and I screamed, punched, slapped and clawed at his face. Carlos didn't hit me – he was after what was between my legs and nothing else. He grabbed one of my arms and held it behind my head. I recall panicking a bit; this wasn't, after all, a 13-year-old girl clouting me in the playground. As he tried to climb on top of me again his hand was inside my knickers and I bit at his arm. He let out a yelp and released me for a split second. I took my chance, managed to lift my legs up to my chest and kicked out at him with all the strength I could muster. He flew through the air and landed in a heap on the grass.

I ran for my life.

He tried to follow but with his trousers around his ankles and an erection I was too fast for him. I made it out of the park and ran up the main road. I spotted a bus, an old fashioned one like the red London buses with an open back platform. Don't ask me how but somehow I was running faster than the bloody bus.

I could hear Carlos behind me pleading with me to stop as I ran my hardest and threw myself onto the open platform. A lady conductor stood at the back and lifted me to my feet. I was in a terrible state, crying, covered in grass stains and mud and my white blouse was literally hanging by a few loose threads. The conductor sat me down and cleaned me up with a handkerchief she took from her pocket as the passengers looked on in amazement. The bus route went past my Auntie Alice's house and I asked the conductor to stop the bus outside her front door. I got off, composed myself a little, knocked on the door and prepared to explain what had happened to me.

She made me bathe and gave me a clean change of clothes, made me a cup of sweet tea and took me back to my Mam and Dad. I was still distressed by the time we arrived and when I saw Mam I broke down and told her everything.

By the state of me they obviously thought I had been raped but I managed to convince them I hadn't. I recall Dad remaining calm and wanting to call the police. I refused point blank. I don't know why. Looking back on the incident, yes, Carlos should have been charged with at least some sort of serious sexual offence. He hadn't raped me but it wasn't for the lack of trying. Hindsight is a wonderful thing and I made a big mistake back then. I only hope and pray that he didn't go on to abuse any other girls but at that precise moment in time the police were the last thing on my mind – the last people I wanted prying into everything, questioning me about the intimate details and events leading up to the assault. I tried to convince myself it was a fight, a fight that shouldn't have happened but a fight that I had won. I didn't even want to contemplate the 'rape' word. It was a horrible word and it hadn't happened. I blocked it from my mind. It was a fight, nothing more.

It brought back the incident with Uncle Tommy a couple of years earlier. I realised if he had tried that sort of thing there was no way I could physically have won that battle. What weird creatures men were. Was it something that they couldn't help doing once they were aroused? I asked myself all sorts of strange questions and began to wonder if this was the shape of things to come as I entered adulthood.

A little later Dad went to bed and I started talking to Mam. She convinced me that this certainly wasn't normal, though men most certainly needed to be watched.

She told me about my granddad that evening as we talked like adults for the first time. Granddad Thomas was gassed during the First World War and came back a changed man. He died before I ever met him. That night Mam told me the incredible tale behind his death.

Grandad was clearly a violent man – but only after the gas my Mam was at pains to point out. He was a lovely man before the war and Mam blamed 'those bloody Germans' for changing him forever. Poison mustard gas was widely used in

World War One as the Germans tried to find new ways of overcoming the stalemate of trench warfare.

Mam said Grandad spoke of the gas attack only once. He described how he crouched in a black mud filled trench as a yellowy-green cloud came drifting slowly towards their line. Before long a pall of dust was all over them – their uniforms, weapons and crudely constructed wooden shelters. As the men began to cough and splutter it was clear that something terrible was happening. What was it? Grandad Thomas stood staring at the incredible scene unfolding before him totally dumbfounded.

'It was a horrible stinking sickly smell,' he'd said, 'it tickled at the back of my throat and made my eyes fill with tears.'

Mam said Grandad Thomas was crying by this point.

'We wanted to get out of there,' he said. 'We knew the gas was slowly choking us and we leapt from the trenches and tried to retreat. As we poured into the next trench no more than 100 yards away, the officers were pointing their revolvers at us calling us a bloody lot of cowards and ordering us to return to the front line.'

'It was either a bullet or the gas,' he said with tears running down his cheeks. He had no choice and returned to take his chances with the gas.

He remembered frothing at the mouth, his eyes bulging from their sockets convinced he was about to die. He pulled a handkerchief from his pocket, tied it tightly around his face and climbed back down into the trench.

By now Mam was in tears. 'He was a lovely man your grandad, he really was but it was the gas you understand.'

He gave Grandma a terrible life after the war and Mam was privy to many a beating Grandma received at the hands of her sick husband (by sick I don't mean he was depraved, I mean he was ill). It was when Grandma died that Grandad grew steadily worse.

'If ever your husband lifts a hand to you, even once our Alice, you make sure you pick up the heaviest bloody thing you can find and hit the bastard with it. Hit him as hard as you can and I promise you he will think twice about lifting his hands again.'

I'd never heard Mam talk like this, never heard her swear before but the attack by Carlos had brought the memories back and here she was giving me a lecture that she had practiced in private over and over again.

She grabbed me by the wrists. 'You promise me that Alice, promise me you'll clout the bugger as hard as you can.'

I nodded. 'Yes Mam I promise.'

Mam explained it was only a few weeks after Grandma died that Grandad Thomas ordered all of his children upstairs. 'You're sleeping in my bed tonight,' he said.

Mam had five brothers and sisters. Grandad positioned them all top to tail in his huge double bed. They thought it was a great hoot but Mam sensed something wasn't quite right. For once Grandad wasn't shouting. He was calm and composed as he tucked them up into bed and positioned himself in the bed next to them. Mam was just about drifting off to sleep when she first noticed the strong smell of gas. She jumped up with a start. Grandad sat upright dozing. 'Dad!' she shouted, 'Dad, wake up, something's wrong.' Grandad remained motionless. 'Don't worry Winnie, you'll all be back with your Mam soon.'

Mam jumped up and ran downstairs to the front door. It was locked and Grandad had sealed the edges with masking tape.

He stood at the top of the stairs. 'Come back to bed, Winnie, you can't get out. Tomorrow we'll be with your Mam. Come on lass, come back to bed, there's a good girl.'

Mam walked back up the stairs and he led her into the bedroom. She described how all of her young brothers and sisters were fast asleep and turning a ghastly shade of green. Mam looked at the bedroom window and noticed that it had been taped up too.

Grandad sank back into bed and his head flopped to the side as his tongue lolled out. Mam believed he died there and then.

Mam picked up the heavy wooden chair and hurled it through the glass window. She described the sheer joy as the cold night air and lifesaving oxygen blew into the room.

Mam saved her brothers' and sisters' lives that night – of that there was no doubt – but my Auntie Ethel suffered from a weak heart for the rest of her life. Mam wouldn't say a bad word about Grandad, she just blamed the Germans and warned me time and time again of what action to take if any future boyfriend or husband ever lifted a hand to me. It was something that would stay with me forever, especially after what I had just experienced at the hands of my so-called boyfriend.

I sat at the breakfast table early the next morning. I hadn't slept well but Mam had made me a little bacon and eggs and a mug of hot sweet tea. It's simply magical, the medicinal powers of hot sweet tea; it's a Mam's answer to everything and incredibly it always works – hot sweet tea makes you feel better.

There was a knock at the door and Mam rose from the table to answer it. She came back into the kitchen ashen-faced a few minutes later.

'It's Carlos,' she announced. 'He wants to apologise.'

Before Mam or I could even react, Dad took control. He sprang from his seat and as he reached the door he turned around. He spoke to me sternly. 'You stay there lass, I'll talk to him. Don't even think about raising your backside from that seat.'

I shook my head. The last person I wanted to talk to was Carlos though I admit he had some nerve coming to the house.

I remember looking out of the kitchen window and watching as Dad and Carlos disappeared up the street. They could have been two best friends walking to the pub. Perhaps that's where they were going to talk things over?

Dad returned after about 20 minutes. He was out of breath but had a strange satisfying look on his face. As I studied him closely I noticed he was a little dishevelled and he had traces of blood on both knuckles of his hands. 'He won't be bothering you again, Alice. I've had a quiet word with him.'

I put the incident with Carlos firmly behind me and despite coming into accidental contact with him practically every week beforehand he mysteriously disappeared from the face of the earth. My God, I thought after a month or two, has

Dad done away with him? He hadn't. I heard from one of my friends that he had been seen in the cafe where we first met. I naturally kept well away from it not wanting to come in the contact with him for obvious reasons.

I never saw him again until I was an adult. I was in my mid-20s, married with a son and if I remember right my boy was at school and I'd nipped into Burnley for some shopping. I heard somebody shouting 'Alicia... Alicia.' There was only one person that ever called me by that name. It was Carlos and I recognised the voice immediately even though I hadn't seen the man for over 10 years.

'Alicia, Alicia it's me Carlos.'

He had changed dramatically. His beautiful shock of black shiny hair had disappeared. He was bald, sporting a skinhead cut. I'm not sure it was the fashion or whether he really had lost all of his hair in his late 20s but it didn't matter. He looked awful, thin and pasty looking and I immediately felt uncomfortable in his company. He tried to reach for my hand but I tucked it in my coat; he was smiling and looked genuinely pleased to see me and immediately started to apologise for the incident all those years ago.

'Alicia I'm sorry. I've wanted to apologise and tell you how much you meant to me and you didn't deserve that.'

Give him his due, he wasn't trying to ignore the incident and a piece of me respected him for even bringing it up. I told him not to worry about it, that it was all forgotten. Carlos told me that he was married and had five children. Bloody hell! There was no holding him back was there!

Carlos begged me to go for a coffee with him so we could

talk about old times. Something told me 'no' and I politely declined and walked away. I never did see Carlos after that; he moved away from Burnley and our paths never crossed again. I couldn't help wondering whether the attempted rape – for that's what it was – was a one-off moment of madness or whether he'd ever had violent tendencies towards other women. A piece of me regrets not taking the incident to the police because I would hate to think that another girl could have gone through what I went through or even worse. I'd like to think that because he was married with five children he hadn't been convicted of anything too serious and therefore hadn't ended up in prison for any length of time. Then again what if his victims had been like me and acted exactly as I had – burying their heads in the sand and refusing to press charges? And what are the statistics in reporting attempted rape cases anyway? Not high I bet. The victim feels a certain sense of relief, almost as if they've been lucky and in my case I believed I'd been in a fight that I'd won.

No, it's far easier to put everything behind you and try to block it out. The 'line of least resistance' they call it.

But it's not always the right thing to do.

CHAPTER 6

Factories and Mills

I decided to knuckle down and concentrate on my career. There was no way was I going to the mill or the factory; it was a career for me, even if I had to move away from home with the words of Miss Baldwin still echoing in my ear.

But it was unavoidable.

I tried for so long to avoid the working direction classmates and friends from our Burnley back streets had taken – the dreaded 'F' and 'M' words.

But within a few weeks I had joined them.

I started work in the local chocolate factory and within an hour my soul had been destroyed. Surely this was not my destiny for the next 40-odd years? I began challenging the working practices almost immediately. My supervisor sat me on a production line of chocolate Brazil nuts. A small conveyor belt containing a never ending row of chocolate Brazil nuts stared up at me. I recalled *Alice in Wonderland*: they seemed to be saying 'Eat me, Eat me'.

The supervisor picked up a chocolate Brazil. 'These are almost ready to be boxed up,' he said. 'Just one thing missing. Do you know what it is?'

I shook my head. They looked perfectly scrumptious.

'We need to put in the ripple effect at the top. We make a little ridge here.' He pointed to the thin end of the nut. 'It makes the customer think the nut has been lifted from a vat of chocolate giving the effect that the chocolate is really thick.' He smiled. 'We call it the "feel good factor".'

He continued. 'Watch carefully, it's your job to give the finished product the ripple effect.'

He licked his finger and gently pulled it around the top of the nut. I gasped. 'You do that with your own finger and spit?'

'I won't tell if you don't,' he said with a grin.

'But isn't there a machine that can do that,' I asked, 'or at least use a cup of warm water?'

'No Alice, spit is better, it's exactly the right temperature, we've tried it with warm water and it goes cold too quickly and we have to keep changing it and therefore we lose production time. Anyway, what are you complaining about – you get free chocolate, don't you?'

I couldn't believe what he was saying. 'But it's unhygienic...' I looked around to see if some of my work-mates were in on the joke. There was no one to be seen anywhere. He wasn't joking. So to all of you enjoying your

Brazil nuts from yesteryear there you have it; you were sucking on some stranger's spit – maybe even Alice Barry's because I've licked thousands of them!

He gave a little wink as he pressed the button and the conveyer belt started and thousands of chocolate Brazil nuts started passing before my eyes. The chocolate was delicious at first but after number 2,672 I didn't want to ever taste chocolate again. As I started to turn green my supervisor brought me a bowl.

He was laughing at me. 'You've done well, Alice; the others turn green far quicker than that. The secret is that you don't swallow the chocolate; spit it into this bowl after every few dozen or so.'

So I sat on the production line for two and a half hours until the first tea break, saving up a gob full of spit which I duly offloaded into the bowl after every 25 nuts. I counted one to 25; I swear it was the only thing that kept me sane. The first tea break was more than welcome, never have I enjoyed a cup of tea so much in my life. But then it was over far too quickly and I was back on the job again licking my finger and rippling another three thousand bloody Brazil nuts until it was time for my lunch break.

Mam had made me a packed lunch with cheese sandwiches, an apple and a Mars Bar. I closed the plastic box. The chocolate covered Mars Bar remained untouched. The other girls or rather the women (they were all much older than me) seemed almost resigned to their fate, content with their lot in life on the production line. One lady said she was a Brazil nut rippler too and that she'd been rippling for almost four years. Her record was just under 19,000 in one day. She held up her index finger with a smile.

It was brown. Oh my God, I thought; no, no, no.

As I went back to the production line I was told to empty my bowl of spit. It was slopping dangerously close to the top of the bowl so I got an unexpected little break as I trooped off to the toilet to empty it. I took as long as I could and made a point of scrubbing my index finger at the same time. My supervisor George gave me a rollicking when I returned. He was looking at his watch and telling me that I was taking too long.

'I needed a pee,' I told him. I held up my hands. 'And I gave these a good wash, cleanliness is next to Godliness.'

His reply was short and to the point. 'Piss in your own time not the firm's.'

He noted something on his pad of paper housed within a clipboard – my first black mark I suspected. Another 2,700 nuts then it was tea break time; 3,000 more nuts and then we could clock off. I'd started work at eight o'clock; it was 5:30 by the time we finished and I was exhausted and somewhat brain-dead.

'Get used to it, our lass,' Dad said as I almost dozed off before tea. 'That's working life I'm afraid. Think of the pay packet at the end of the week. Then it will be worth it I can promise you.'

That night I dreamt of Brazil nuts. Evil little monsters with slitty eyes and an evil grin as they jumped from the conveyor belt and chased me into the toilet. Just as they were all about to attack me I woke up bathed in a cold sweat and then realised it was a dream. I looked at the clock. In little over an hour the bloody Brazil nut nightmare would start all over again and I hated the little bastards.

By the end of the week my production was up to nearly 15,000 and two bowls of spit a day. I wish to place on record that I have not eaten a Brazil nut for over 40 years, not even at Christmas time. And Dad was wrong, the wages didn't compensate at all for the hours and hours of lonely purgatory I was suffering.

I couldn't go on much longer.

I think it was the loneliness that was the worst – having no one to talk to on a day to day basis. The highlight of the working day was lunch time where I could sit down with my fellow zombies, recharge my brain and check that my tongue and lips were still in working order.

I made it until the end of week three before I eventually cracked. I stopped the conveyor belt and swept about 40 Brazil nuts onto the floor where I stamped on them with unadulterated glee. My supervisor hauled me into the office and read the riot act to me, threatening me with dismissal. I didn't care. I told him that if I saw another Brazil nut I'd take up a sharp bread knife and slaughter the entire workforce.

George, my supervisor, appeared to mellow a little and asked me what was wrong. I explained that I was lonely and I needed someone to talk to and something a little more stimulating.

'I've just the thing for you,' he said as he stood up and walked towards the door. 'Have you heard of "Sooty" and "Sweep"?'

'Yes,' I replied. 'Hasn't everyone?'

'Then come with me, we'll let you work with Sooty.'

He's lost it, I thought; he's a by-product of the Brazil nut production line. He's flipped his top, no doubt about it.

I followed him outside his office and groaned as he pointed me towards yet another conveyor belt just outside his office, where he could no doubt keep an eye on me. But this was better, there were other ladies around the conveyor belt and instead of chocolate Brazil nuts a little line of chocolate Sootys tootled along quite happily. One lady applied three black chocolate buttons down the front of his yellow coat while another gave him eyes and another a nose.

He excused one of the ladies and I took her place on the production line. He smiled as he told me he was giving me a big responsibility. 'You can give him his wand.'

I kid you not, my dear reader; my position of responsibility was to give Sooty a little candy wand in his tiny hand that he held up with a convenient hole another lady had poked out earlier in the production process while the chocolate was still soft enough. Promotion, I thought to myself – hallelujah! – and not a bloody Brazil nut in sight.

At least the Sooty belt was bearable up to a point as I could at least share a laugh and a joke with the other ladies. After a while helping Sooty with his magic wand became second nature as we talked about everything and nothing and even held little trivia quizzes to keep our brains active. I still watched the clock of course and couldn't wait until the end of the working day but at least we had a little fun to break up the monotony of Burnley factory life.

I'd been on Sooty's line for about three weeks when George started picking on me for talking too much.

'You're not paid to talk Miss Blackledge,' he'd shout at me and I'd go quiet for a while before the overwhelming urge to natter took over again. He took me into the office a few times and threatened me with Brazil nuts but I'd argue that however much I talked the production line would run at the same speed and Sooty never ever came off the end without his magic stick.

'You don't like me do you?' I asked him one day. He just shrugged his shoulders and told me he wasn't paid to like or dislike people. As long as they did their job that was all he was interested in. He sent me back out to work again, but this time placed me on an Easter egg production line. The Easter egg belt was equally as dull and boring as every other conveyor belt in that horrible, horrible factory. It was full of Easter egg halves which we had to weld together. Beside each seat was a small machine not unlike a flat iron. We took two halves of Easter eggs and held them on the machine, not too long and not too short, just enough time to melt a tiny layer of chocolate and then we'd place a packet of sweets inside and melt them together and place them on a different belt which would take them to another set of girls who'd box them up. Talk about brain dead – it was enough to make you reach for a rope or a sharp knife.

I worked with a lady called Peggy. She was quite a bit older than me and always game for a laugh, keeping me entertained during the long hours of mind-numbing monotony.

We had a small locker room in the factory where we went each evening to remove our overalls. Peggy turned to me one night and said, 'Do I look alright?'

It was a strange thing to say and I looked her up and down and said, 'Sure Peggy, you look fine.'

She pointed at her ample breasts. 'Here Alice,' she said, 'here look at my bra, do you notice anything unusual?'

I stared at her chest for a second or two, unsure what it was I was actually looking for.

'You look fine Peggy,' I repeated. 'It's a pair of breasts, rather a large pair I'll give you that but they look about the same size to me and I'm sure your husband considers himself a lucky man.'

Peggy laughed and pushed me hard in the shoulder. 'You daft bat,' she said. 'Watch carefully.'

She closed the door that led direct to the factory slid the lock along then turned to face me. An evil grin spread across her face and she began to unbutton her blouse. My God, I thought this was it. The factory lesbian is coming on to me. I began to protest as she opened the front of her blouse and exposed her ample bosom. She reached around the back and began to undo the clasp of her bra.

'No Peggy, you've got this wrong. I'm not like that...' I began to wail.

But wait, something didn't look quite right with that bra. It was oddly shaped and little bits of brown stuff poked out the side.

'Abracadabra,' she announced with a grin as she held half an Easter egg high in the air.

I still didn't get it. What was Peggy doing shoving Easter egg halves into her bra? Was it some sort of perverted fetish and was it something I was missing out on, yet another fact of life that no one had bothered to explain to me?

'They are for the children,' she explained with glee. 'They get chocolate every night do my kids.'

And then it dawned on me. Peggy was nicking the Easter eggs – only two mind, or rather one because remember we had to weld them together. It was a well thought out operation that Peggy had perfected every Easter and it had kept her children in chocolate for more years than she'd care to remember. It took about five minutes for the chocolate to melt so she had to be quick in order to remove them from her breasts at the bus stop just outside the factory gates. Genius, bloody genius. Who would have thought of that?

I wasn't destined to be one of the longest serving workers in the chocolate factory. My days were numbered but to the best of my knowledge Peggy's scam was never discovered. Good luck to her, I say; I just hope her children got plenty of exercise and didn't grow up too fat!

I've already mentioned that the highlight of the working day was lunchtimes. How sad is that? After a little spot of lunch some of the girls would take a cat nap (power naps, I might add, weren't officially invented until the year 2000!) They'd climb up onto the sacks of cocoa beans which were stacked on top of each other some 20 feet high. I swear they were the most comfortable beds I had ever slept in; in fact the person who invented the beds that mould into the shape of your spine must surely have been on the production line of a chocolate factory and experienced one or two kips on top of the cocoa bean sacks.

They were so comfortable that one day I crashed out for nearly four hours. George eventually found me as they scoured the factory convinced I'd been sucked into one of the huge vats of chocolate.

He went crazy with me and docked me a whole day's pay.

From that point on the writing was on the wall. I lasted another two weeks before he called me in and told me he was putting me back onto the Brazil nuts.

I told him to stick his Brazil nuts up his backside and walked out there and then.

I was terrified at the thought of facing up to Dad but as always he told me that I didn't have to do anything I didn't want to. 'There's plenty more factories and mills, love,' he said. 'A clever girl like you won't be out of work too long.' Aren't Dads great?

He was right. Within a week I'd started an apprenticeship as a weaver. At least I think it was called an apprenticeship. The entire month's training was delivered by a frustrated masochist called Edna. Nothing was ever good enough for her and to be quite honest with a week or two's instruction a five-year-old could have worked the machine known as a 'loom'.

Edna used to hit me if I did anything wrong; she'd hit me with the approval of the other supervisors and the management at the mill. Back then it was normal to dish out physical punishment to the 15 and 16-year-olds fresh from school. Imagine that happening these days?

Edna wore a pinny and had a huge bosom which quivered when she shouted at me. I'll say something for her she was definitely passionate about her work and her machines, and watched over me like a hawk. The looms were huge pieces of apparatus with cables and wires strung across that pulled the cotton back and forth, eventually creating the material for sale. The atmosphere in the mill was one of oppression and exploitation, and the theory that the worker gave his or her pound of flesh was in full flow. It was essentially a sweatshop.

Edna hit me if I went too slow and hit me if I went too fast and got my hook caught up in the threads which stopped the machine. Edna hit me across the back of the hands and knuckles with a solid wooden shuttle, a device that made up part of the machine. It was shaped like a child's bath time boat about six inches by four. Just when I thought I was getting the hang of it, Edna would step in and admonish me, wielding her shuttle which she held in her hand permanently. Whilst she never broke any fingers I remember an occasion or two where she actually drew blood.

I qualified to run my own machine after a few weeks but still Edna wouldn't leave me alone hovering over me like a praying mantis. Eventually I snapped, telling the old bat if she didn't leave me alone I would walk. We had a head to head with one of the managers who had witnessed my capability on the loom and was of course more interested in his productivity bonus. He thus gave me my own machine.

Edna was furious and still struggled to keep her distance (deep down I think she loved me like one of her own daughters...maybe not!) She was never far away from my machine and I could still hear that voice of hers and the dull thud of the shuttle as she brought it down on some poor unfortunate's knuckles.

I remember the day she stood no more than 15 feet from me shouting at a girl who had been working just a few days. She hadn't hit the girl yet but my experience told me it wasn't far away. She snatched the hook from the girl's hand and yelled at her that she was the most useless apprentice ever to have graced the factory floor. I smiled; she said that to me as well and as the girl's bottom lip trembled I made a mental note to tell her at the next break. Events, however, took a change of direction. Edna leaned over the loom to demonstrate the correct method. I remember looking at her pinny as it hovered over the fast moving machinery and wondered if perhaps Edna's breasts were dangling oh so dangerously near.

I wanted to shout that she was careless and unprofessional as the first of her breasts got caught in the machinery. She squealed like a stricken pig as the second one followed soon after and because of the size of her breasts the loom locked solid and froze with a loud screech.

Edna was panicking and clearly in excruciating pain as she tried to pull herself free. I suppressed a laugh at the irony of Clarkson's Mills greatest loom instructor trapped by the tits. I shouldn't laugh, I told myself, but I did, I laughed for England as I crumpled behind my machine with my hands clamped tightly around my mouth.

A team of engineers were drafted in as they dismantled the

machinery around her breasts as she begged them to be gentle with her. I'm not sure what was worse for poor Edna the pain she experienced or the sheer indignity of the situation as several young men groped and pulled at her breasts for well over half an hour, cutting away the entire top half of her clothing including her bra exposing her mammoth mammaries to the world. I swear every man in the factory from the managing director to the floor sweepers appeared at some point during the on-going operation to take a sneaky look at Edna's tits feigning sympathy and offering technical solutions to the problem.

They eventually managed to free poor Edna, though I suspect her husband's sex life suffered for some months thereafter.

I recall the sheer look of orgasmic ecstasy on Edna's face as the second breast was finally released. I assumed at the time that Edna would take a backseat, mellow a little as she trained her new girls. Sure, we all made a few mistakes with the fast moving machinery, but no one had made such a huge faux pas as Edna.

But I was wrong. If anything it made Edna even more bitter and twisted as she took a kind of sadistic pleasure with her new recruits.

Meanwhile life in the mill was beginning to get me down.

There have been many occasions in my life where there has been a final straw (that incident in the girls' toilets at school, for example) and sure enough I sensed my time in the mill was destined to end. The cotton on the looms was tinder dry and the friction of the machines, if not cooled down occasionally, they caught fire. It was quite a common happening – perhaps once or twice a week. More often than not the flames on the machines were extinguished fairly quickly, but on this occasion a through draft breezed across the factory floor and as I looked on in horror the flames jumped from one machine to the other. The mill floor was filled with acrid smoke as people ran around in a panic, throwing buckets of water here there and everywhere.

That was it…I was off.

I ran out of the mill coughing and spluttering, climbed the stone steps that led to the front street, and gulped in the welcoming fresh air. They brought the flames under control quite quickly and I sat on the steps outside watching the smoke gradually disappear. I was glad of the little break as I sat in the sunshine but then my impromptu rest was rudely interrupted by the supervisor who called me back inside.

'You did not have permission to leave the factory floor,' he shouted as he thrust his fingers in my face.

'But the place was on fire!' I said incredulously.

'That's no excuse.'

'I couldn't bloody breathe!'

'I don't care,' he yelled. 'You don't leave the factory floor without permission.'

I reached behind my back and untied my protective apron. 'No?' I said. 'Then just watch me do it again.'

I threw the apron at him, waved a hand in his face with a sarcastic expression and walked away. As I reached the door he shouted at me to return immediately.

I turned around and faced him. 'Stick your mill up your

arse!' I said. I'd never been more certain of a decision in my entire life. I'd reached the conclusion that factories and Alice Blackledge just weren't meant to be.

CHAPTER 7

An Accident and Mental Anguish

Poor Mam had worked in a mill for nearly 20 years, albeit a different one from the one I walked out on.

She was responsible for replacing the large cotton reels in the jute mills. She'd walk around several machines and watch carefully as the reels ran out of cotton. When she could see the bare wood of the reels she'd spring into action carefully replacing the near empty cotton reels with a full one. It was quite a skilled job and of course the machines never stopped during this process. An idle machine was lost production, and although a little dangerous, the machines had steel grill guards that prevented a stray finger from getting caught up in the gears and cogs.

Occasionally a guard would fall off and an engineer would be found as quickly as possible to stop the machine and refit the guard. If an engineer couldn't be found the machine would not be stopped. Idle machines equalled lost production and the supervisors would advise the operators to take care.

I'll never forget the day of Mam's accident. I'd just arrived home from work as Dad was rushing out of the front door. He said Mam had had an accident at the mill and we had to go to the hospital. As we sat on the bus, he explained that Mam's hand had been dragged into a machine and wrapped around the gears and cogs like a piece of meat. It had been mangled beyond all recognition and it was some time before someone noticed and stopped the machine. Dad had been sent for but someone also had the good sense to send for the local factory inspector – the modern equivalent of the health and safety man.

For some bizarre reason I can still recall the name of the factory inspector – Mrs Blackburn. She caught the engineer desperately trying to fix the safety guard onto the blood-spattered machine.

Meanwhile Mam lost her arm from the elbow down.

The doctor said that every finger had been snapped, with two lost completely in the workings of the machine and every bone in her wrist broken too. Her radius bone had been broken in 17 places and the tendons and veins severed beyond repair. We were allowed in to see her before the operation to amputate her arm but she was so drugged up she didn't even recognise us.

The mill was in trouble and had broken just about every rule in the book. Whilst Mam was still in hospital a local solicitor visited Dad grinning like a Cheshire cat and offering to represent us, promising riches beyond our wildest dreams.

Mam came home after a couple of weeks. She was a different woman and it affected me badly; I soon followed her into a deep depression. I couldn't imagine what she had gone through – the pain, the agony whilst the machine continued. She never talked about the accident but the solicitor described with glee how one by one her fingers had been torn off or snapped like twigs as the machine slowly dragged in her wrist, mangled it up and inch by inch swallowed her arm. The solicitor said that it had taken more than an hour to free her and that the pain she was in was simply unimaginable.

'More pain means more money,' he told my Dad.

Understandably Mam couldn't work again. The thought of going anywhere near mill machinery was something she couldn't face.

I never did like the look of the solicitor though he was right, the eventual pay-out was huge. The only problem was that the money ended up in his client account and he refused to give it to us. After a couple of years we did eventually receive less than half the actual compensation amount; the solicitor had conned us and siphoned off the bulk of the money into his own bank account. Dad took legal advice and although the solicitor was eventually struck off and jailed, the money was gone.

There was, however, enough money to buy a house said Dad one evening and I remember that surprised me somewhat. He smiled as he told me he had a nice place in mind.

Things happened quite quickly after that with dad visiting a lawyer several times to finalise the legal requirements. It was exciting, of course, but also a little daunting. We were moving out of the only house I'd ever known and relocating to the other side of town leaving our special street and our many friends behind.

It was around this time that Dad started opening up to me. He asked my opinion on things and at one point even told me about his duty in the Second World War. Mam had talked about it a little because her brother Tommy Clemensen had been captured near Dunkirk and spent five years in a German prisoner of war camp. The Germans set him to work in the mines because that had been his profession before the war started, eventually making him a supervisor. Tommy would ultimately spend five years in the concentration camp before the Germans took him to hospital with a brain tumor. In an ironic twist of fate they operated on him, removed the tumour and saved his life. Tommy survived the war and came back home to Burnley when he carried on a normal life for many years. Although Dad and Tommy discussed the war only rarely I remember one or two occasions when dad would wind Tommy up, telling him he should have been a faster runner so he could have escaped from the Germans. Tommy used to laugh it off, telling Dad it made no difference to him working in an English mine or a German one, and that he had fared much better than the silly buggers dodging bullets in northern France. I think Mam's brother Tommy had a great deal of respect for the Germans; he didn't witness the many horrors of war but Germans had saved his life.

As a schoolgirl I didn't think Dad was involved, which was a little stupid of me because every man of his age had been conscripted unless they were in a reserved occupation. I knew that the miners were a reserved occupation and I assumed because Dad worked for the Coal Board he would be in the same boat.

He wasn't; he was an infantry man and one of the soldiers rescued from the beach at Dunkirk. There were never any photographs of Dad in uniform in our house and Mam never talked about it either. It was fresh in the memory back then and I think they just wanted to forget about it, just like everyone one else who'd been touched by the tragedy of war one way or another. It took over 15 years before he even mention the word 'war'. We would be sitting in the kitchen in the evening with Mam upstairs in bed and he would start talking. Dad tried his best to keep the family together and although he wasn't depressed I would describe him as quite melancholy. He only told me two stories about the war but he would repeat them over and over again. His eyes would glaze over and he'd stare into space when he described the scene unfolding on the beach at Dunkirk. The Allies were in disarray with their tails between their legs and running for home. The German army had cut the Allies in two in northern France. Dad said that many of his friends in his regiment had been either killed or taken prisoner by the Germans. He described himself as one of the lucky ones who had made it to the beaches of Dunkirk and had to wait to be rescued by a flotilla of boats on the way from the southern coast of the United Kingdom. They were beaten and dejected, and because the Germans were still shelling the beach area, they had to wade into the sea, hoping the shells would cause less damage when they landed on water. He described many shells landing close to him in the sea and how there was insufficient impact to detonate them. Some exploded, of course, but like Dad said, he was lucky. I can't imagine what that must have been like to watch a bomb dropping from the sky towards you and simply praying that the shell would sink harmlessly to the bottom of the ocean. Winston Churchill described the invasion in the House of Commons as a 'colossal military disaster' and even though the officers at the time did their best to keep the Allied troops' spirits up, Dad and his comrades were convinced that the war was over.

There were 200,000 British soldiers rescued towards the end of May 1940 and Dad was one of them. He described a line of small boats as far as the eye could see. But there was no joy or pleasure as he climbed aboard a small fishing boat that would take him home; he sat there thinking about his dead and wounded colleagues lying on the beaches and the mainland of France. His rescue boat bobbed in the sea which had turned a deep crimson colour as dead bodies floated helplessly on the surface. Dad recalled thinking to himself that the fish in the English Channel would be well fed for many years to come.

I sat in silence as he relayed that story, the tears welling up in his eyes, and I always thought he would break down and sob as it drew to a conclusion but he never did. He was a strong man – a man's man – and it was as if he was drawing on strength from deep inside him to continue through to the next battle which was to save his wife and his family. He thought that if he could recount those dark times – the worst time of his life – and not crumble he could face anything that civilian life could throw at him.

He told me another story, this one even more horrifying because it described perfectly the way war affects men who are thrown into conflict. As far as I can remember he only told the story once or twice, three times at the very most and generally when he'd had a couple of beers that lowered his defences, and somehow stripped something away so that he could tell me. I remember the first time very clearly: I think Dad had been to a funeral or perhaps visiting a very sick friend in hospital. Death was on his mind and he was looking sad and depressed as he nursed a cup of tea at the kitchen table. Mam was poorly again and upstairs in bed. There was just me and him and I asked him if he wanted anything to eat. He shook his head, said he didn't feel like eating. We sat in silence for quite a few minutes and I knew he had something to say.

'He was only 17,' he whispered, '18 at the most.'

I was confused. 'Who was 18, Dad?' I asked.

Dad looked up. There were tears forming in the corner of his eyes as he spoke.

'We shouldn't pass judgement Alice, war is a terrible thing and men are pushed to the limit.'

Dad was back in Dunkirk again. I kept quiet as he told the story little by little. I bit my lip 100 times conscious that if I butted in the tale would never be told.

'We were watching from a forest, about half a dozen of us who had been cut off from the main group. The Germans didn't know we were there. They were clearing out an old barn full of Allied prisoners. We would later find out they were making them ready to be moved to POW [Prisoner of War] camps in Germany and Poland. There were at least 100 German soldiers, well-armed and well-disciplined, and at least another 20 to 30 SS soldiers. It would have been sheer suicide for the six of us to get involved.'

Silence. *Keep your gob shut, Alice, for once in your life.*

'Prior to this incident we thought we were doing well in the war; we'd cut the German line in half and were advancing towards the east. It was probably the only part of northern France where we outnumbered them. But this was a whole different kettle of fish. I think it was at this point I realised we were losing.'

Dad took a long slow drink from his tea cup and gulped it down in one. He wiped at a tear that started rolling down his cheek and his bottom lip began to quiver.

'We'd heard rumours about what the Germans had been getting up to, particularly the SS men, and we were frightened. We'd seen their divisions and their soldiers and their armaments and their trucks and their tanks as we watched from elevated positions or camouflaged hideaways in the forests that ran alongside the main roads.'

Dad looked up. 'We were frightened, Alice. Everyone was frightened.'

He paused for a long while. 'If the truth be told we were absolutely petrified. The SS had formed a sort of gauntlet outside the barn and our lads came out waving white handkerchiefs above their heads. The SS threw a few punches and well-aimed kicks and hit a couple of our boys with rifle butts. Two of them crumpled in a heap and fell to the floor.'

Dad pulled a handkerchief from his pocket and blew his nose as he continued.

'There were only two of them, Alice, one was a man about my age in his mid-20s and a young kid no more than 18. A couple of the Germans gave them a rough time – nothing too sinister; they screamed and shouted at them and landed a couple of punches to the head and face. Like I said, war changes men. I remember looking in the young boy's eyes: he was terrified, like a rabbit caught in the headlights of a car, trembling like a leaf. One of the German sergeants ordered them against the barn door with their hands above their heads. They obeyed without question.

'The other prisoners were tied up and could do nothing to help. There were about a dozen prisoners, no more; two or three of them appeared to have been beaten quite badly, black eyes, broken noses that sort of thing. I remember looking over towards a truck and seeing the body of a Canadian paratrooper riddled with bullets and I feared the worst for the two boys that had been separated from the rest of the group.'

By now Dad's tears were flowing freely and he was speaking very quickly. It was clear he needed to get this off his chest.

'None of the prisoners were resisting, they were all resigned to their fate, which at that time we believed was a year or two in a prisoner of war camp at the very most. But as I looked on it was clear that the Germans were separating the other two prisoners from the rest and an eerie silence fell over the scene. The SS seemed to take over proceedings, herding the bulk of the prisoners towards the trucks and leaving the other two isolated by the barn door.'

Dad looked up, his eyes were full of tears and his cheeks shiny and wet.

'The poor bastards knew, Alice. They knew they were going to get it.'

That was the first and I think the last time I'd heard my father swear. It just wasn't done in those days, fathers did not swear in front of their daughters.

'When the sergeant first placed his revolver to the young lad's head, I thought he was play acting. The young lad didn't though. He started crying, begging for mercy though I don't suppose the German knew what he was saying.'

Dan held his teacup tightly in his hand. It was cold by then and he squeezed it so hard I was convinced it was going to shatter into a thousand pieces.

'I have never seen so much fear in anyone's eyes, Alice.'

I reached out and levered his fingers individually from the cup and placed it on the table. He never reacted, he simply stared into space.

Dad took a deep breath. 'He pushed the barrel of the gun against the poor lad's temple as he begged for mercy and pulled the trigger.'

And then Dad broke down and sobbed like a baby. Between the tears he told me not to blame the Germans, that war was wrong and it changed men. Yes, he'd hated the assassin at the time and would have gladly run from the forest and torn him apart with his bare hands.

'But who knows,' Dad shrugged. 'He had his orders, no

doubt, and one killing in front of a large group of men might leave them in a permanent state of terror, might just prevent an uprising at a later date. War changes men, Alice, it hardens them; just remember that and try not to think too badly of the poor soul who pulled the trigger.'

God knows what poor Dad went through on Dunkirk beach and yet it was that incident that prayed more on his mind than any other.

Dad talked a little more about the young lad who was killed that day, about how he had his whole life ahead of him and probably didn't even want to be there in the first place. He talked about his grieving parents and family members, and he shed more and more tears for the boy. I suspect Dad would have taken to the grave the image of the sheer terror on his poor face. And yet despite all that Dad also had a little sympathy for the German assassin who probably didn't want to be there either.

That was Dad. Caring, protective, compassionate.

And here he was nearly 40 years later, still the same caring, compassionate man and protecting poor Mam like a week-old kitten.

I hoped that the move to the nice new house would cheer both Mam and me up but she was never the same again. She was so brave and yet understandably the accident had changed her whole personality. Every week she attended the hospital at Preston where she was eventually fitted with a false arm. She would come back and say that she was the lucky one. 'Losing my arm is nothing compared with some of those poor people in there,' she'd say.

At times she seemed more concerned that she'd lost her wedding ring. The machine had ripped it from her finger and chewed it into a dozen pieces. Mam had always been busy in the house – cleaning, baking cakes and biscuits several times a week – but after the accident she was no longer at ease in the kitchen and spent long periods sitting in an armchair staring into space. Watching her like that tore me to bits.

I spiralled deeper into depression and at the end of a long, long weekend I'd had enough. Mam sat in the armchair and nodded as I told her I was going for a lie down. I climbed the stairs, went into the bathroom cabinet and reached for a full bottle of aspirins. I couldn't watch her any longer. It was the only way out. I was going to kill myself.

I don't know how many pills I took that afternoon but I remember munching them by the handful. The taste of the aspirins was sweet and sickly and by the time I had finished the bottle I began to feel a little drowsy. I lay back on my bed and closed my eyes. It was all going to be so easy, so peaceful. Killing yourself wasn't such a big deal.

Luckily for me my father somehow sensed there was something not quite right. Alice Blackledge did not normally take to her bed on an afternoon.

I vaguely remember him coming into the bedroom. 'What's up with you?' he said. 'Are you ill or something?'

That's when he noticed the empty bottle of pills by the side of my bed. Dad went absolutely mad lifting me from the bed and carrying me downstairs.

He ran to a neighbour to telephone an ambulance and was

back within a flash ranting and raving at me. I felt he was about to give me a crack at any minute such was his temper. I don't remember an awful lot of the trip to hospital only that the ambulance had its siren on and I drifted in and out of consciousness. My stomach was pumped by the local hospital – a procedure I would not recommend to anyone. 'Gastric irrigation', as it's called, is the method of eliminating poisons from the stomach. A tube was pushed into my nose and eventually found its way into my stomach. It was sheer agony. Normally they use a little lubricant to ease the process but on this particular occasion someone apparently decided I was going to suffer and suffer I did. Small amounts of liquid are then pumped into the stomach, triggering automatic vomiting. What a bloody mess. I daresay I was a little out of it when this process took place but nevertheless it remains with me like a horror story and I would never want to go through anything like that again.

Within a few hours I was more or less conscious and well enough to go through to a ward. Dad had been at my bedside during the whole period. Why on earth had I put him through something like this? By this time I was beginning to think clearly again and couldn't believe how stupid I'd been. The nurse explained to Dad that I was fit enough to go home but then she said the local constabulary had turned up wanting a word with me. The police!

I'd committed a crime, the nurse explained; suicide was against the law. I was absolutely shitting myself. I was already thinking about the sin I had committed in the eyes of the Catholic Church and the guilt was beginning to get to me in a big way. Not only did I now have the police to contend with – my Dad was next in line!

I think I was more frightened of Dad's ultimate reaction than the police and the Catholic Church put together. Fathers hit their children in those days and I was convinced that I was in for the mother of all batterings. I was already feeling really low and I had now come to terms with the magnitude of what I had actually done. I felt selfish and guilty, and I thought about poor Mam and the suffering she was going through. I looked at Dad and noted a mixture of fear and sadness in his eyes. How could I have done that to him, how could I have been so selfish? I could just about understand that trauma he was going through with his wife as I'd been affected that way too. He'd fought hard trying to keep his family together and just about remained sane; now his daughter had tried to commit suicide. What on earth was he going through?

The police were really quite pleasant and I recall a very young police woman talking to me quite softly. She asked me if I had attempted that sort of thing before but I assured her it was definitely the first and last time I would do such a stupid thing.

I kept one eye on Dad who sat in the corner of the room while they interviewed me. It was surely only a matter of time before he erupted like a volcano. I remember the concern etched on his face and how sad he looked. Why had I done this to him I asked myself over and over again?

After about 20 minutes the police left; they seemed reasonably satisfied with the interview and the hospital eventually bade me goodbye. My God, the beating I was about to receive was now surely only a few minutes away. I was terrified as we stepped out into the hospital grounds but Dad just walked slowly on ahead. When we got to the hospital gates he turned round to face me and put his hand on my shoulder.

This was it.

'Listen, Alice,' he said, 'I'll tell you what we're going to do. We are going to call in at that nice cake shop on the way home and pick up a box of cakes.'

Cakes? I thought. *Cakes?* And here was me expecting a clout, not a cake.

'We're going to go home, make a pot of tea and sit with Mam and eat cakes all day. We are going to have a little chat and then we are going to put this behind us and after today we'll never talk about it again.'

I stood with my mouth wide open, nodding at him like one of those nodding dogs you sometimes see on the parcel shelves of cars.

'Just promise me you'll never do anything like this ever again.'

Then he put his arms around me and gave me a big cuddle and I sobbed like a baby. That's how wonderful Dad was and I miss him every day. I miss him too much for words.

CHAPTER 8

The WAAF and Pontins

There wasn't such a thing as a Job Centre in those days or a careers office, just a dole office where the unemployed signed on. That's where you also went to look at a notice board where the factories and mills posted the latest vacancies. Textile manufacturing in Burnley started way back in the 14th century but it was during the second half of the 18th century that the town established itself as one of the country's most prominent mill towns. At its peak, it became one of the world's largest producers of cotton cloth and Burnley Loom was recognised as one of the best in the world.

The town was quite prosperous and there was never any real shortage of jobs. Most of the young people finished school one day and started working the next.

I recall standing in the dole office once again scanning the notices and sighing. As much as I tried to fight it I knew being born in Burnley meant the mill or the factories.

I was back staring reality in the face again. You left school and took a job. 'A job for life' I remember the teachers telling one boy. You worked from the age of 15 until you were 65, retired and if you were lucky had a few years as a pensioner doing nowt before dying.

What was wrong with me? The jobs simply did not appeal and my experiences of mills and factories up to now hadn't exactly been pleasant ones. The thought of spending eight or nine hours a day in that type of environment seemed like a fate worse than death. But there were dozens of jobs on that board and I was expected to earn my keep. I couldn't hide forever.

I jotted down a few addresses and references and pushed them into my pocket; I'd send off a couple of letters when I got back home. On the way back home I bumped into my school friend Marjorie Leesen. She was so excited and couldn't stop talking about her new career. A career, I thought – not a job. She mentioned the name of the company, the WAAF.

'What mill is that?' I asked. I'd never heard of it.

'Don't be stupid,' she said. 'It's the air force for girls – the Woman's Auxiliary Air Force.'

Suddenly I saw a way out. No way was I going into a factory or a mill.

The Royal Air Force. Brilliant! I would see the world and get paid too. I reached into my pocket and pulled out the

Above left: Me and my cousin Annie at our Holy Communion.

Above right: My mother.

Below: My mum, brother and sister.

Above left: With Terry on our wedding day – the toothless bride!

Above right: With my sister.

Below: Celebrating 25 years' service at Holdings Café.

Above: Me and my siblings.

Below: My son Terry's wedding.

Above: Me with Jim Broadbent.

Below: Me and Terry with Danny Boyle.

Above: With Graham Norton.

Below left: With Willem Dafoe.

Below right: Me and Jeff with our mate Ciaren Griffiths.

Above: Me and Pat Mancini, the 'Queen of Blackpool'.

Below: At *Phoenix Nights*, with Roy Walker (*left*) and Peter Kay (*right*).

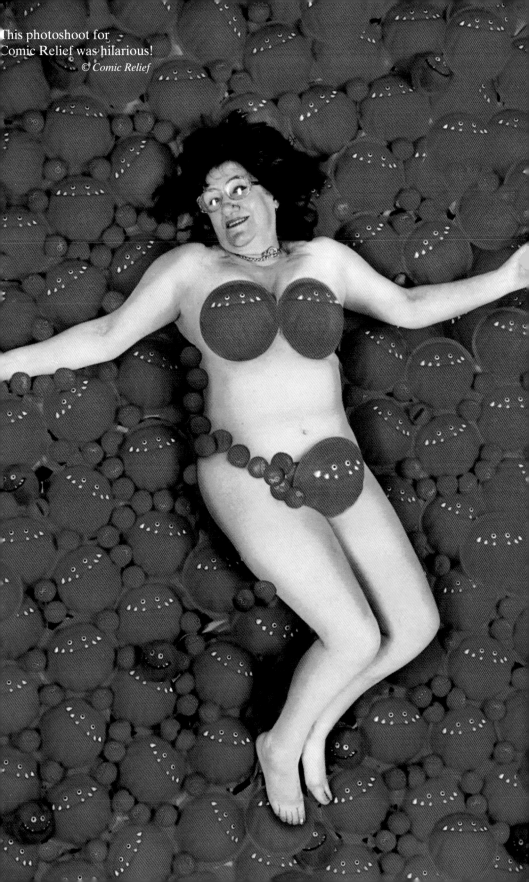

This photoshoot for
Comic Relief was hilarious!
© Comic Relief

Above: Our showbiz launch party for Barry's, with the 'Who's Who' of comedy.

Below: With Mikey North and Shobna Gulati

© *Manchester Evening News*

scraps of paper I had written on in the dole office, tore them up, and threw them into the air.

'Where do I sign up?' I asked her.

Marjorie told me to calm down. There was an IQ test for new recruits each Friday at the recruitment office in town.

'You have to be a little bit smarter than average,' she said.

We went together to the office in Finsley Gate where we were welcomed by a lady officer, a Leading Aircraft Woman all dressed up in her fine blue uniform complete with cap. It all looked so exciting and glamorous, with recruitment posters on the walls and models of huge aircraft suspended from the ceiling. This was it; this was a real *career*, not just a bloody job!

We sat the test along with another dozen or so girls, and although it wasn't easy I felt quietly confident that I'd answered most of the questions correctly. I jumped for joy two days later when I received a letter in the post inviting me for an interview and medical. Marjorie had passed her test too and we went for the interview together. I was in there for no more than 15 minutes and the Leading Aircraft Woman smiled as she told me there and then that I was exactly the sort of young enthusiastic person the WAAF was looking for. I think she was telling me politely that I hadn't shut up during the whole interview! Marjorie grinned like a Cheshire cat when she came out of the interview room and gave me the thumbs up. We were in, both of us. Just the formality of a medical.

I proudly announced to the doctor a week later I that had never had a day off school in many years. I wasn't asthmatic or diabetic, didn't have a heart condition or flat feet and I had never undergone any medical operations. I was confident. As the Leading Aircraft Woman had said I was exactly what the WAAF were looking for.

So how was I to know I had a bloody lazy eye? What was a lazy eye anyway, and what was the big deal – couldn't it just work a little harder?

In medical terms it is known as 'Amblyopia', a disorder of the visual system that affects about five per cent of the population.

'I am sorry,' the doctor announced. 'I'm afraid you won't be joining the WAAF.'

Bugger, bugger, bugger.

Of course Marjorie breezed through the medical, didn't she. Good luck to her, I thought – it mustn't have been meant to be. I tried to remain positive and wished her all the best. If life throws you lemons, make lemonade. I'd get over it. But deep down I was distraught.

I remember the discussion with my mam and dad. 'I'm going to work at Morecambe,' I announced. I remember Mam saying '*Morecambe?*' with a puzzled look on her face. 'But you can't go to Morecambe, our Alice, it's miles away, how will you get home for your dinner?'

'It's okay,' I said proudly. 'The company are providing me with accommodation.'

Dad looked from behind his evening paper. 'And wages too, our lass?'

I nodded.

I explained the company was well respected, a good employer and it was a career for life (that bit was a fib).

'What's the company called?' Dad asked.

'Pontins,' I replied.

Mam smiled. 'Well I never, our Alice working for Pontins!' She got up and gave me a big hug. 'No factories for *my* lass,' she said with a big smile on her face.

I'd escaped the dreaded factory and the mill. Alice Blackledge, a career girl! As I packed a small bag the night before I was due to leave I suddenly remembered I'd never really been away from home before, not since staying with Auntie Ethel in Lancaster some years back.

I thought I was the bees' knees when I went shopping with Mam in town to buy my bits and pieces for my big adventure. She bought me toiletries and a new hairbrush, new underwear and a couple of other items of clothing if I remember correctly and insisted on paying for everything even though I had a few pounds of my own. On the surface Mam seemed so happy that day, and quite proud that I had secured a position at Pontins. It was a big deal in those days, believe it or not, to get a job with a company like Pontins. Hundreds and hundreds of people applied for each position and only a select few were ever successful.

I was more than a little proud of myself as Mam and Dad waved me off at Burnley bus station. I had my own small suitcase and a magazine I'd bought for the journey. This was it, this was the start of Alice Blackledge's career and I was determined to make the most of it.

It started well and I was greeted at the front gate by one of the supervisors. She told me no one worked on the first day and proceeded to show me around the camp.

'Your first day is for you to find your feet,' she explained. 'Get your bearings so that you know where everything is.'

She led me into the canteen. 'First you have to eat,' she said. 'Your meals are free and you can eat anything you like – but be careful or you'll pile the pounds on.'

She introduced me to Patrick, one of the cooks. 'Patrick will get you a little breakfast,' she said, 'and then you can start to explore. Have a nice day; have a nice season at Pontins.'

Patrick must have thought I looked ill because he cooked me a breakfast that would have fed six navvies! He was lovely and he smiled at me while I ate. I may have been mistaken but I'm sure I saw a glint in Patrick's eye – the type of glint that makes men want to show you their willies…

I had applied to Pontins via a job application form and had indicated that I felt I would be suited to a position in entertainment. I wrote that I would be a natural with the children and felt my skills would be best put to use working with groups, keeping people happy and generally organising games and events.

They gave me a job as a chalet maid.

Although I was disappointed at first, it didn't make any difference to my enjoyment and my new-found independence. We worked hard – it was a nine-hour day starting at seven o'clock in the morning with a long break at lunchtime – but when we were finished we were free to do whatever we wanted. We went to the beach, used the swimming pool and mingled with the guests. At night we went to the bar on site or sometimes ventured into the town.

I became really friendly with a girl called Maureen who had a really bad stutter. She had a husband in the Navy and she talked about him constantly and worried about him all the time. The memories of World War Two hadn't altogether disappeared from people's minds and Maureen had a theory that somehow Adolf Hitler would rise from the dead and it would start all over again. I constantly reassured her that those days were over and nothing would happen to her husband.

Patrick was always hovering in the background and now and again he came out with us. Maureen told me to stay away from him, that he was bad news and it was rumoured that he was looking after at least three or four girls on the camp. 'Looking after' – that's a new one, I thought.

I went back to my chalet for an early night one evening after a red-hot day of swimming and sunbathing. I was dead beat. I had just turned into bed when I heard a key turning in my lock – the next thing the door swung wide open and Patrick stood there grinning, holding two bottles of beer.

My immediate reaction was to ask him how the hell he managed to get into my chalet. He held up a key ring with 100 different keys swinging from it.

'I can get into anywhere,' he said. 'I have keys for all the chalets; it's part of my job.'

Patrick walked in and sat on the edge of my bed. I knew what was coming. It was willy time as sure as eggs were eggs.

Patrick leaned forward and tried to kiss me, but I turned

my head and slapped his face. I can still see the look of shock on his face to this day. This had clearly never happened to him before. He shook his head in bewilderment as he rubbed his cheek.

'You've got the wrong idea about me,' I said.

He stuttered struggling for words. 'But all the girls here are...'

'Easy?' I finished his sentence for him.

I pointed to the door. 'Not this one, Patrick.'

Give Patrick his due, he was a gentleman after that. He apologised, handed me a bottle of beer and left rather meekly with his tail between his legs. After that I slept with a chair wedged behind the door but Patrick never bothered me again.

I caught up with him the next day and he apologised again. We had coffee together in the canteen and he told me that one day he wanted to meet a girl that he truly loved and respected, and that he wanted her to be like me. I suppose that was a thinly-veiled compliment and I fully expected a follow-up line asking me out on a date. But it never happened. I liked Patrick and I would never hold his attempt to get me into bed against him. It was just his big clumsy way of trying to come on to me. Not too subtle, I admit, and not very stylish either. But Patrick, if you're reading this, I hope life has treated you well over the years.

Three or four weeks into the summer season my Auntie Sarah turned up for a 'day trip' (or so she said). I knew that Dad had sent her to keep an eye on me. I don't know what she expected to see on a day trip as most of the shenanigans went on at night, but I kept my nose clean throughout the day, knowing that Sarah would take a good report back to Dad.

Six or so months later I was working with Maureen in a chalet close to the swimming pool when one of the supervisors appeared in the doorway entrance.

He looked at Maureen. 'There is someone to see you in reception, Maureen. I think it's quite urgent – you need to come quickly.'

Maureen panicked and reached for my hand. 'There is something wrong, I know there is!' She begged me to go to reception with her, fearing the worst. Her panic attack was infectious and I remember trembling and shaking slightly as we approached the reception door.

Just as we got there a tall handsome man in a naval uniform appeared in the doorway and started running towards us. It was Maureen's husband. As he reached us he picked her up and began swinging her around, kissing her. Her hair shook loose and his cap fell to the ground and I'm convinced music started playing in the background and everyone in the near vicinity froze and watched as this magical scene unfolded before our very eyes. This was all before the movie *An Officer and a Gentleman* but I'm convinced that one of the young campers that day at Pontins in Morecambe must have been none other than Taylor Hackford, Hollywood director, and that that moment stayed with him until he met up with Richard Gere and Debra Winger on set in 1982.

After a few minutes Maureen came over to me and announced that she was leaving. Her husband was taking her away and she wouldn't be back. He said he had other more important things on his mind after being away at sea for over 12 months – the mind boggles!

I never did see Maureen again but I'm sure just like the movie Maureen and her handsome husband lived happily ever after. Or at least that's what I like to think.

After the season I was back home in Burnley. I'd enjoyed the experience and the independence but I was bitterly disappointed that despite doing everything that had been asked of me, they'd decided to terminate my contract. As I sat on the bus back home I tried to put it behind me. I muttered my life-long motto all the way back to Burnley: 'what's for you won't pass you by'. Pontins was a little step of experience on the long staircase of life and I'd loved every minute.

Mam and Dad were so pleased when I announced that I was home for good. Our home may have lacked the material things that other families had but I never wanted for love and I always, always felt welcome. My parents could not disguise their joy that my Pontins adventure had come to an end.

CHAPTER 9

Love, Sex & Marriage... In That Order!

It was around about this time in my life that two monumental things happened to me. I was offered a job that I would settle into for the next 18 years and I received a proposal of marriage. I was 19 years of age when I was offered the job, at Holden's café in Burnley Market Hall, but more of that later.

I'd known Terry Barry and his family for some time and to tell the truth I'd always had a soft spot for that giant of a man with a seemingly permanent smile fixed upon his face. Both of our families were at our friend Herbert Stacey's wedding in the local church hall. I'd ordered a drink at the bar when six-foot-four Mr Barry sidled up to me and asked if I was enjoying myself. I told him it was a marvellous affair and we shared a few pleasantries. Then he stunned me.

'I like weddings, Alice,' he said. 'How about me and you getting married?' He showed me Herbert's marriage lines. 'How about me and you having some of those?' he said. 'We'd make a great couple and to be honest with you I've had my eye on you for some time.'

I laughed, making some sort of wise crack about hardly knowing him, and yet my heart was beating 20 to the dozen.

'What are you talking about? We've known each other for years,' he said. 'C'mon Alice – let's get married.'

He was serious. I looked into his eyes and this crazy man was actually serious. My heart was still pounding and although I half expected him to crack up any minute and tell me he was joking, but he didn't.

I told him it might be a good idea to have a few dates first. He agreed (thank God) and we started courting. From that very first evening we were inseparable and the relationship worked like a dream.

Terry was the first boy to awaken my sexual feelings. Although I'd had one or two dates with other boys and a few stolen kisses in the back row of a picture house I'd never really had the desire to take it any further. As you are aware I'd also seen my fair share of willies too, but that's as far as it went. I'd looked but hadn't touched!

Terry was a man, a full ten years older than me, and he smelled like a man. Does that make sense? He lived with his mother, a kindly old soul but she was almost stone deaf and deeply religious (and I mean *deeply* religious). I sometimes thought early on in our relationship that Mrs Barry only approved of me because I was a practising Catholic like her and her son. I was in no doubt that if I'd been born on the other side of the fence – that is, the Protestant fence – she wouldn't have accepted me quite so easily. As it was, from the beginning I was welcomed into the family like a daughter and made to feel at home.

Mrs Barry had no concerns about leaving Terry and me alone in her house. After all, we were good Catholic people.

Every Wednesday evening without fail she went to Benediction at the local church. Although Terry and I attended Sunday Mass together we weren't so religious as to feel the need to go to church during the week, apart from the odd confession.

But we loved Wednesday Benedictions because it meant Mrs Barry was out of the way for at least two hours – which meant we could get on with other things. We'd turn on the radio or put a record on the gramophone and snuggle up on the settee for a marathon snogging session. That was as far as it went. There was never any question of sex before marriage and the moral instructions and preaching of the priests were always uppermost in our minds. It was the best birth control known to mankind.

Most of the time, anyway.

Mrs Barry had left at the usual time. I remember it was a bitterly cold evening and Terry had banked up the fire. The room was rather hot and I remember removing my woollen cardigan, and Terry took off his jumper, as we kissed for what seemed like ages. I was getting hot and bothered in more ways than one when Terry suggested we go somewhere a little cooler and more comfortable. His mother's big double bed was the obvious choice. The room was cool and the sheets pleasant against the skin as we fell on the bed giggling.

'Not a word of this to Mam,' he said.

As if.

Our natural feelings took over and gradually we cast off our clothes, exploring each other's bodies as if it were the most normal thing in the world (which it was).

Within a short time we were totally naked and Terry lay on top of me. He took over. I was a virgin and my big gentle giant introduced me to one of the most wonderful things on God's incredible planet. I never thought about the consequences at the time and of course we hadn't planned to have sex so we didn't use any form of birth control. Not that we could have anyway; we were both practising Catholics. One of the more ludicrous instructions that has been handed down from Rome for nearly 2,000 years is that birth control goes against Biblical teachings and that it is always intrinsically wrong to use contraception to prevent new human beings from coming into existence. This includes sterilisation, the Pill, condoms and even the withdrawal method.

But I wasn't even thinking about birth control as I lay back in the bed, breathing gently and bathed in sweat, believing I loved this man more than heaven itself. I turned to face him to tell him just that when I heard the front door bang.

Mrs Barry was back.

Shit, shit, shit!

Terry was in a state of shock as he reached for his clothes and I remember him freezing momentarily as he looked at me totally starkers. 'You've taken all of your clothes off!' he said.

Isn't that what you're supposed to do? I thought to myself. During the heat of the moment I'd stripped myself naked. I think Terry had expected me just to lift up my skirt and at the very most remove my knickers, and he was genuinely stunned as he stared at me in my birthday suit.

We broke the world record for getting dressed and smoothed the bed down as best we could. It was damp and sticky and I prayed that it would be dry before Mrs Barry climbed into it later that evening. *This couldn't be happening!* I thought to myself.

However we had a more pressing problem. Most of the houses in Burnley at that particular time were two-up two-down – that is to say they had two bedrooms upstairs and a lounge and a kitchen at ground level. The pressing problem at that particular time was how Terry was going to sneak me out of the house through the lounge without Mrs Barry noticing. Her catching the two of us upstairs and knowing what we had been up to was something that I just could not face.

We listened to Mrs Barry's movements from upstairs. We could hear her footsteps walking towards to the door that led to the stairwell. She opened the door and called out for Terry. He answered her, he said he was at the toilet and would be down in a minute or two.

What was I going to do? I couldn't stay up there the whole night. We hatched a plan.

Mrs Barry was nearly stone deaf. The only way Terry could get me out of there without her noticing was to distract her for a minute or two so that I could get out of the front door.

Oh no, I thought to myself, the first time you have sex shouldn't end like this. I wanted to lie back in my lover's arms, caress him and stroke his hair – not run around playing hide and seek!

Terry went downstairs and told his mother I'd left some time ago. I lay on the bedroom floor with my ear pressed to the rug. I could hear Terry making small talk with his mother. I bided my time.

After a few minutes Terry opened the door at the bottom of the stairs and whispered to me to come down.

I crept downstairs and he explained that he'd get his mother to make a cup of tea. When she went into the kitchen to boil the kettle he'd give me a sign and I could dart through the lounge to the door that led to the street outside.

Tell me this isn't happening, I said to myself, please tell me this isn't happening. But it was and miraculously our cunning plan worked.

I heard Terry ask his Mam to put the kettle on and then I heard her little footsteps padding across the linoleum flooring.

Terry let out a loud cough. That was my signal and I was off through the lounge quicker than Linford Christie. I ducked down as I walked past the lounge window outside and then I was off running through the streets as quick as my legs would carry me.

I lay in bed that evening feeling a little pleased with myself but also a little confused. I knew now that I loved Terry more than life itself and wanted to spend the rest of my days with him but I had also committed a cardinal sin in the eyes of the church. I thought about Father Murphy. Oh my God, what would he think if he knew that I had participated in sex before marriage?

Should I confess? I thought for a fleeting second or two? Not a chance – what on earth did it have to do with him?

The following day Terry and I met up after work. He asked me if I remembered what he'd said during that meeting at our friend's wedding, when he handed me the marriage lines and said we should get married. He went on to say that he meant every word of it and after the previous night he felt we had another very good reason to tie the knot. As marriage proposals go it wasn't the most romantic in the world, but Terry was Terry and it was the best I was going to get; besides I could see in his eyes that he sincerely meant every word.

So we chose a date. We wanted to get married as quickly as possible. We settled for 7 March 1962, Ash Wednesday – the earliest day the church could accommodate us. It was no more than six weeks away and we would have got married even quicker if it had been possible. We had originally opted for Lent week but the church was full.

It was so exciting, yes I was only 19 but I felt ready for it. I talked to Mam and Dad about it and they were as excited as I was. We discussed a wedding dress but the truth of the matter was Dad didn't have the money. He was working for the coal board at the time but there were long periods where he would be out of work. Any savings he managed to put to one side were simply eaten away during the periods of unemployment. Poor Dad, I really felt for him – he would have given me his last penny but he didn't have two of them to rub together.

About a month before the wedding Mam came in with

some good news. One of our neighbours' daughters, Kath, had been married six months previously and said I could have her dress. Mam showed me the dress. It was a beautiful brilliant white – but it was considerably larger than I was. I latched onto that as an excuse but the reality was I didn't want to wear anyone else's dress for my wedding. Mam tried to convince me that the dressmaker would do a wonderful job but I dug my heels in and eventually she gave up. Wedding dresses were ridiculously overpriced, I thought, so I made do with a black-and-white two-piece patterned dog-toothed suit and a white half-moon hat which cost a fraction of what a wedding dress would have cost. To this day I regret not having a white wedding – it was something I really truly wanted – but it was not to be.

Then there was the pre-wedding meeting with Father Murphy. I'm not sure if this still goes on these days (I suspect it does) but both Terry and I were told after church one Sunday that we needed to make an appointment to see him before the big day. It was all very solemn and serious – almost like a confession – only this time we weren't confessing anything, we were there to be lectured on sex and babies. My friends had warned me and I can tell you there were some crazy rumours flying around. One of my girlfriends even joked that the priest would demonstrate sexual positions to us. As if I'd believe that one!

Father Murphy sat us down in the front pew of the church and pulled up a chair, positioning himself no more than three feet away. He had the full cassock and dog collar on; this was official, nothing too informal.

He was very serious and started by telling us it was our duty as good Catholics to bring up all of our children in the Catholic faith. That was expected, no big surprises there. Then he stared at us as if we were something the cat had dragged in. He raised his voice a decibel or two and twisted his face showing genuine disgust.

'You haven't had sex yet, have you?'

It wasn't like a question, more like a statement, a directive, a command to warn us that if we were thinking about it we were to rid ourselves of those evil thoughts.

'No, Father,' I said.

'Wouldn't dream of it, Father,' Terry said.

All I could think of was our explicit forbidden act, first on the rug in front of Mrs Barry's fire and then upstairs in bed. I pictured Terry's perfect naked aroused form. *Stop!* I screamed to myself. I had to banish those thoughts, make them go away. Part of me was thinking that Father Murphy might be able to read my mind.

At last Father Murphy spoke. 'Good, I'm glad to hear it.'

He believed us?

He turned to me. 'You must *never* use birth control, Alice, and I don't want to hear that repulsive word "condom". Sex is for making babies, not for enjoyment. Sex is a sin, an evil wicked act.'

We nodded in unison. I wanted plenty of children – four actually.

'And only in the missionary position,' he continued. 'Is that clear?'

'Yes, Father Murphy.'

We couldn't get out of there quick enough. I was absolutely mortified that I'd lied barefaced to a priest in the presence of God Almighty. It couldn't get any worse, could it? Surely nothing could be worse than what we'd just been through?

I was wrong. A fate worse than death for a young bride was ready and waiting. Lurking in the shadows. The next day, with just three weeks to go before the wedding, I visited the dentist. My teeth were something that I really took care of. They were brilliant white and straight and I religiously cleaned them three or four times a day and even paid the dentist to polish them regularly (something quite rare in the early 1960s). I remember making an extra special effort that day and I stood in front of the mirror cleaning them for what felt like an eternity.

Mr Stavely, the dentist, was smiling as I walked into his surgery. With all the horrible mouths that he had to look inside, mine must have made quite a pleasant change. But during his examination he pulled a piece of cotton from my mouth and it was covered in blood. He stood back with a worried look on his face.

'Oh, Alice,' he said. 'There's quite a bit of blood there; has this been happening regularly?'

I told him I had noticed blood occasionally on my toothbrush after I had cleaned my teeth, but I thought it was because I'd been pressing a little too hard.

'No,' he said shaking his head. 'I think it's a little bit more serious than that.'

He continued to examine me and took various swabs from

the corners of my mouth, pressing quite hard on several teeth. Each time the swabs were covered in blood.

He walked over to his bench behind my chair and then returned. Very matter-of-factly he said 'I'm sorry, Alice, but you have pyorrhoea.'

'Pyo-*what?*' I said

'Pyorrhoea. It's a disease of the gums and it's very serious.'

I remember lying back in the chair wondering what treatment I would have to undergo and whether it would be painful. The doctor was explaining what the disease actually did to the gums and how my teeth would eventually drop out one by one.

'So what's the cure and the treatment?' I asked

The dentist was shaking his head. 'I'm afraid there isn't any cure, there's only one treatment.'

'And what's that?'

'I'm going to have to take all of your teeth out.'

I sunk back into the chair. I thought I hadn't heard him correctly but he was nodding his head.

'*All* of them?' I asked

'I'm sorry Alice, yes, all of them and the sooner the better.'

I explained I was getting married in three weeks' time. He told me not to worry, that he would have my false teeth ready by then.

False teeth – just before my wedding!

I was devastated and I don't know how I ever made it out of the surgery. I didn't take a bus home – I walked, unable to take in the news. Surely there had been some sort of mistake; surely something could be done?

What would I tell Terry? Would he still want to marry me? This wasn't fair, this simply wasn't fair. Was it my punishment from the Lord for having sex before marriage? All sorts of ludicrous thought were flying through my head.

I went home and told my parents. They said it was quite common and that the dentist was right – the only treatment was to have all of my teeth out. He'd been very thorough, the dentist, checking every one of my teeth. I remember him pushing and pulling at each one individually.

I went back to the surgery the next day. I don't know why but I asked to speak to the dentist again and he confirmed that it hadn't been a big horrible nightmare that I'd dreamt up. The disease had spread right through my mouth, top gums and bottom gums, at the front and at the back. He smiled as he told me he could fit me in within a few days. My name was entered into his diary and I started thinking about what I was going to say to Terry.

I was a nervous wreck as I sat in front of Terry, babbling on about stuff that made no sense. Eventually I spat it out. He took me in his arms and squeezed me tight. 'You stupid girl,' he said. 'I'm marrying you for what you are not what you look like. I love you,' he said, 'I love you with all my heart and I'm marrying you and walking you down that aisle whether you've got teeth or not.'

It was probably the worst thing Terry could have said. I blubbered like a child thinking I was the luckiest girl in the world to have found a man like that. I still wanted to put the wedding off but he wouldn't have it and convinced me that we'd have a great day. Despite my protests he convinced me that it was for the best and pointed out that many arrangements had already been made that couldn't be broken. I went along with it; God knows why but I went along with it. I would be walking down the aisle with false teeth and I just knew that I'd look like a perfectly acceptable caricature of Bugs Bunny.

The next day I went to the dentist and he removed all of my teeth. I knew nothing about it as I was under the effects of laughing gas. I remember going under and counting to ten. That was a horrible feeling in itself as a mask was placed over my face and I breathed in the foul-smelling substance.

Nothing could have prepared me for what I would face when I came to. I was aware of the overhead lamp gradually coming into focus and the dentist talking to me. He was speaking softly and smiling; 'Everything is fine,' he said. The pain hit me immediately and grew steadily worse throughout the next few minutes. It was as if somebody had taken a hammer to my face. My jaw hurt, my head hurt and even my ears screamed out for mercy. What on earth had he done to me? I attempted to speak. I didn't know what I wanted to say but I just tried to speak. The words didn't come out – instead a river of blood flowed from my mouth, splashing onto the protective bib spread across my chest. I panicked and gagged as I burst into tears. The dentist was telling me not to worry, that everything gone according to plan and although I would be in pain for most of the day it would subside by early evening.

The dentist and his assistant proceeded to clean me up and wouldn't let me leave the chair for at least 20 minutes. I recall asking for the mirror several times but my request was always denied. The young dental nurse said it would be better if I looked in the mirror back home. She said my mouth was terribly swollen and there wasn't an awful lot to see. The lying bitch. She knew what my reaction would be and clearly didn't want to be there at that precise moment.

I placed a scarf over my face as I walked outside and made my way to the bus stop, managing to mumble my destination to the bus driver. I held the scarf over my face and started crying; the pain was excruciating and I could feel my whole face swelling up by the second. I think the bus driver managed to hit every bump between the dentist's surgery and our street and I was so relieved when I made it to the front door.

Mam and Dad were waiting for me and were obviously curious about how the operation had gone, but I refused to take the scarf from my face. I went to bed and cried myself to sleep. I knew what I would look like but it could wait until morning. Mam ventured up an hour or two later with aspirin and warm tea. I still had the scarf on my face and drifted off into a fitful sleep.

It was about seven in the morning when I made my way to the bathroom. I will never forget that moment as I stood and looked in the mirror. Alice Blackledge wasn't in the bathroom that day, instead a stranger stared me in the face. An ugly stranger, a stranger with no teeth, puffed-up swollen fish lips and eyes that were black and blue and tearful. My delicate cheekbones and soft features had gone and my head looked twice its normal size. My face was yellow and purple, and a mixture of congealed blood and snot was fixed firmly in place across my top lip. I remember wondering how could anyone kiss a face like that and how could anyone walk such an ugly specimen down the aisle. Thank God I was getting false teeth.

I ran a bath and made an effort to clean myself up.

I refused to see Terry until I had my false teeth. A week passed and at least the swelling had gone down a little as I made my next trip to the dentist. The scarf was almost permanently attached to my face but the pain had gone. He took measurements of my mouth and made soft wax casts. Everything was perfect, he said – 'I'll have you looking like a model when you walk down the aisle'. God love him – he was trying his best but I just wanted my old teeth back.

It was just over a week to our wedding and Terry had insisted on seeing me. I expected a reaction, a look of horror when he set eyes on me, but Terry just looked like Terry. There wasn't a flicker of emotion in his face, let alone a look of disgust, and then the big soft bugger kissed me like he had always kissed me, with tongues and all! Wasn't I the luckiest woman in the world?

I received a letter from the dentist the following day advising that my teeth would be ready two days before the wedding. Talk about cutting it fine. The letter explained I wouldn't be able to wear them permanently as they would be a bit a bit painful and my gums would need to adjust accordingly. I didn't care. If I had to walk up the aisle in abject agony I was ready for it. It was my wedding day and I would be smiling like a Cheshire cat!

It was a Monday afternoon when I went to collect my

teeth. Of course I had my scarf with me but promised myself I'd shove it in the nearest bin as soon as I came out of the surgery. I was sick of that scarf and it smelled of dried blood. It was the only scarf I had and I hadn't dared wash it for over two weeks.

The receptionist ushered me into the surgery and as soon as I looked at the dentist's face I knew something was wrong.

'I don't know how to tell you this, Alice,' he said, 'but your teeth aren't ready.'

My worst nightmare had come true. In two days' time I would be getting married. My family and friends would be there and every eye in the house would be fixed firmly on the toothless bride. I wanted to run away and hide. I didn't want to be married. I asked the dentist if there had been some misunderstanding; surely the teeth would be there tomorrow?

'No,' he whispered quietly. The technicians in Manchester had a backlog and were several days behind. Wild horses couldn't bring my teeth to his surgery – they would be at least another week, possibly as long as ten days.

It was the end of the world for me. It was my wedding day and I was supposed to look at least half nice. I'd accepted that I didn't have a wedding dress, I could just about live with that, but no bloody teeth?

My God, how on earth did Terry talk me into it? But he did. He took a day off work on the Tuesday and more or less begged me to go through with it, telling me how much he loved me and that he didn't care what I looked like. How could I have let him down?

The night before my wedding I visited Grandma. She was a real old character and I don't think I ever saw her without a floral pinny. I'm sure she had been sewn into it. I can still picture the scene as she stood by the black lead fireplace tapping her fingers on the top ledge.

'You must never refuse your husband when you're married, Alice,' she said. 'Men are men and nature is nature and they have their urges that need fulfilling.'

She took me gently by the shoulder and leaned in to me as she spoke in a whisper. 'Never refuse your husband, Alice. Otherwise he'll cast his coal in someone else's cellar.'

That was the sort of saying she used to come out with and I still laugh when I think of her to this day.

The next day I was married. I was Mrs Alice Barry. I don't think I smiled the whole day for fear of someone catching me on camera but deep down inside I was ecstatic, the happiest girl on the planet, and at times I almost forgot about my teeth – or rather the lack of them. We couldn't afford a posh official cameraman, of course, and that was a blessing in disguise. Imagine if we'd forked out all that money for nothing. The Lord works in mysterious ways.

Something strange happened as Dad got ready to walk me down the aisle. He turned to face me and I thought he was going to tell me to remember to keep my gob shut. He smiled at me and the tears welled up in his eyes as he spoke. 'It's never too late, Alice. You don't have to do this. If you don't want to go through with this just tell me.'

I was shaking my head but he continued. 'You don't have to do anything you don't want to. I love Terry and his family but you're my daughter and my first born and you are the only thing that matters to me.' I gave him a kiss and a cuddle.

'No Dad I'm happy and really sure about this. I wish I had some teeth and a bloody wedding dress but life can't always be perfect.'

He took hold of my hand and squeezed it and we started to walk.

I enjoyed every minute of the service; it meant so much to me and of course at that time I was what the church calls 'devout'.

Just before I turned to walk back down the aisle as Mrs Alice Barry the priest stopped me and planted a big dirty mark in the shape of the cross in the middle of my forehead. It was Ash Wednesday and a wooden cross had been burned earlier. It was a tradition that had to be adhered to.

What on earth did I look like? I had to be the ugliest bride ever and yet no one seemed that bothered, especially not my gorgeous husband.

I think the priest would have been bothered though, or rather he would have been if he'd known I was pregnant. I wasn't 100 per cent sure at the time but I'd noticed the subtle changes in my body. I'd convinced myself that it was all part of adulthood. Things like that were never discussed with your parents and the sex education side of school was non-existent. Of course we talked about sex, pregnancy, periods and contraception at school and in the workplace, but there were so many different stories you didn't know which ones to believe.

CHAPTER 10

Cancer

I visited Mam and Dad several times a week when I was first married. It was difficult to break the family ties and anyway I didn't want to. However, that first time I went, after the wedding, after our honeymoon, after Terry and I had practised our fair share of sex (and not just in the missionary position...) I couldn't even look Dad in the eye. He knew what I had been getting up to – now that I was Mrs Barry – and the idea that he knew what his little girl had been doing was very difficult for me. Yes, I was entitled to do it now that I was a married woman, but the whole act was somehow dirty and sordid to me. I'm not surprised, because that's what I had been fed for some 20 years. It took me some weeks to get over my guilt so that I could relax totally in Mam and Dad's house.

Dad still treated me like his little girl and as I sat in the comfort of the family lounge I sometimes had to pinch myself to remind me that I lived somewhere else. Although Mam had changed since her accident she nevertheless still retained her special character and funny traits which rose to the surface every now and then. She would look in the kitchen quite regularly and say 'It's like a bloody padding can in there,' meaning the room was upside-down. I'd ask her what the hell a 'padding can' was but I swear I never got an answer. I sincerely believe the internet is one of the greatest inventions in history. Pre-internet I'd struggle to grasp the meaning of Quantum Physics or be at a loss to find out the exact geographical location of the Great Wall of China but not now. However it's not entirely infallible because not even our friends at Google can establish what a padding can is. Anyone who knows, drop me an email at my fan club site, alicebarryfanclub.com!

I have, of course, saved the best until last. We'd be rowing, as most mothers and daughters do occasionally, and I'd be answering her back, and she'd stand with her hands on her hips and frown at me. And then the immortal line would come out... 'You don't care a no never mind, you!'

What?!

At first I thought she'd simply got the words the wrong way round but then she'd repeat it.

'You don't care a no never mind, you.'

The bizarre thing is I knew exactly what she meant. The sentence made no sense whatsoever but I knew exactly what she was trying to say.

Mam was always ready to offer a little gem of a story when needed. Okay, at times she was mad as a box of frogs, but nevertheless I wouldn't have swapped her for the world (p.s. I was just trying to be clever about Quantum Physics, I know nothing about what it is nor am I interested!)

There was also one piece of advice that Mam drummed into me time and time again as I matured towards adulthood, especially during the run-up to my wedding and the first few weeks of married life. I remember her going over the story about Grandad and the gas many times and how he'd badly used our Grandma. Mam explained that being married was part of a big game and if you got the rules right at the beginning then the marriage could be long, happy and successful. If not you could end up like poor Grandma – a downtrodden, insecure, battered old punch bag.

'Look for the signs,' Mam said. 'Look for the first signs of violence and then hit back as hard as you can.' She held me gently by the arms as she looked into my eyes. She was deadly serious, quivering with emotion. 'As soon as he lays a hand on you, Alice, promise me you'll hit back and hit him with anything you can. I promise you he won't lay a finger on you ever again.'

I was telling my Mam not to be so stupid, Terry wasn't like that, he wasn't a bully, he wasn't violent like other men. At this point I had been married only a matter of days.

Mam was nodding. 'That might well be the case, our Alice, I'm just telling you to be on your guard.'

Mam looked strange, her eyes wide open and penetrating and her face was a ghastly pale shade of white. She looked terrified – terrified for me. Poor Mam had let her little daughter go and she was absolutely petrified.

Some weeks after the wedding I began to show a little and went to the doctor's to take a pregnancy test during which he confirmed the good news. I say 'good news', because it was; Terry and I were absolutely ecstatic. We'd talked about children and wanted a large family. We jumped for joy when I arrived home with the results of the test. We couldn't wait to tell everybody and rushed out that same evening to our parents' houses and shared the good news with our brothers, sisters and close family members. The following day we told our friends and work colleagues.

A few evenings later I was standing at the sink washing a few dishes. Terry wandered into the kitchen and put the kettle on. 'I'll give you a hand with those dishes,' he said. I protested. He'd only just arrived home from work and looked absolutely shattered. 'Sit down,' I said. 'I'll do them.'

Terry wouldn't have it; he sidled up to me at the sink and began nudging me. 'Move over,' he said. 'Let me in, I'll do them.'

Terry was just play acting, though I didn't know at the time. All I recalled was my mother's warning about domestic violence and how I should react to it. Terry was nudging me harder now, pushing me out of the way. 'Move!' he said forcefully and I snapped. I thought about my grandmother and how she had been the victim all of her married life.

I was washing a cast iron frying pan at the time. I remember tipping the water out into the sink, grabbing the handle with both hands, and swinging it through the air as hard as I could. I even had to jump up to hit him he was so tall.

As soon as it connected with Terry's skull I knew I had made a huge mistake. What was I playing at? He was trying to help me with the dishes, for God's sake. Terry collapsed onto the floor, the blood gushing from a large split in his forehead.

I couldn't apologise enough, begging his forgiveness right there and then in the kitchen and en route to the hospital where they inserted fourteen stitches into a head wound.

I explained what my Mam had said and told him the story about my grandad.

'But Alice, I'll never ever lift a finger to you, surely you know that?'

I did know it and yet Mam's words had preyed on my mind.

Thankfully Terry's wound never left a permanent scar but it took many months before it gradually disappeared completely. Every time my eyes were inextricably drawn to it I cried a million tears inside. How could I do that? How could I hurt my big gentle giant?

And Terry was as good as his word; he never lifted a finger to me until the day he died.

Terry Barry Junior was born in on 21st September 1962. We were the proudest parents in the world. He was christened in St Mary Magdalene's Church seven days later. Father Murphy presided over the service. Father Murphy looked so pleased – after all he'd christened me, watched me grow up into a young Catholic woman, educated me in the ways of the church and eventually presided over my marriage ceremony.

I attended Mass regularly and even cleaned the church three nights a week – gratis, of course – and here I was starting all over again with my child who would no doubt grow up as I had done with the church being the focal point of his existence.

And then Father Murphy's face changed – it changed in an instance as his smile disappeared and turned into a scowl. He had figured it out, put two and two together and at that precise moment he'd done the mental arithmetic. He had married us only seven months prior to the christening of our child. The innocent-looking girl who stood in front of him had completely ignored his teachings and his advice and of course the words of the Scriptures. She'd had sex before marriage. The Jezebel!

As we stared at each other for a few very uncomfortable seconds I knew that he knew and he knew that I knew that he knew. My face flushed red. We stood in silence for a minute or two before he continued. I squirmed with embarrassment throughout the rest of the service.

Give Father Murphy his due, he never mentioned it again but I can honestly say that my relationship with Father Murphy and the Catholic Church was never the same. It's difficult to explain – it's as if I felt I had a penance to pay to the church and the guilt feelings were back with a vengeance. I had sinned *big style*, or at least I had in the eyes of the Catholic Church.

I hadn't regretted my sexual encounter with my husband-to-be. I wasn't proud of it, but it wasn't something I was ashamed of either. I'd known for a long time that Terry was the one who for me and it was a natural progression in our relationship that seemed right at the time. Human nature. After all it's God that made us and therefore God who must have given us the urges and feelings; it's all part of the human instinct to reproduce. And that beautiful consenting act ultimately produced the most wonderful bundle of joy – our precious son.

It was meant to be, it's as simple as that. I was deeply religious in those days but my views on the world have changed somewhat over the years. Now I find it difficult to comprehend what the Bible teaches me – that the world was created by intelligent design some 4,000 years ago and in only seven days. (Six actually, because the Old Testament tells us the Lord rested on the seventh day). Visiting the Natural History Museum in London and physically setting eyes on dinosaur bones and fossils that are millions of years old it's difficult to take the literal meaning of the Bible at face value. And yet even now I remember Terry's birth as it was only yesterday and I remember looking at his perfectly formed little body, which his father and I had produced during the wonderful act of love, and I sincerely believed back then that it was a gift from God and that something as physically perfect as my young infant could not have evolved by accident. Someone had to have made him and that someone was God. Like I say, my view on the world has changed and there is so much the Catholic Church instilled into me that I find difficult to swallow. I want to believe in evolution and Charles Darwin's theory and the Big Bang and yet...well, you get the picture. I still pray every night of my life and I think that should tell you something.

We were just a few years into our marriage when we decided to move to Lancaster. It seemed like a good idea at the time; it was less than 30 miles down the road and a lot of our friends lived around the town. We hadn't been there that long when Terry came in from work one day with a worried look on his face. He'd found a small lump on one of his testicles.

Terry being Terry he shrugged it off. It wasn't painful, he said, probably nothing. By pure coincidence I had an appointment that day at the doctor's and I badgered Terry to come along with me. Rather reluctantly he agreed and we took the bus to the doctor's surgery. I explained to the receptionist that Terry required an appointment too; those were the days when you could turn up at a doctor's surgery and be seen without an appointment, you didn't need to plan an illness in advance!

We sat in the waiting room and Terry's name was called first and he walked away from me. His examination seemed to take forever but eventually the door opened and Terry walked back through. I remember him looking a little pale and I was just about to ask him how the examination had gone when my name was called over the waiting room tannoy. Terry told me to go through and he would speak to me afterwards.

It was a day I'll never forget.

I walked through the door and then into the practice

room of our family doctor, the same doctor who had examined Terry.

His head was bowed looking over some notes as I announced my name. He seemed momentarily stunned and looked a little flustered as he fiddled with his notes. He had put two and two together and realised that I was Terry's wife.

He stuttered, looked a little embarrassed even.

'I'm sorry,' he stated sternly and without emotion. 'But I'm not the sort of doctor who minces his words. I tell it how it is,' he said.

I shrugged my shoulders; 'I don't understand.' I said. 'What are you talking about?'

'Mr Barry is your husband isn't he?'

'Yes,' I said. 'What about him?' What's wrong with him?'

'You need to get your affairs in order,' the doctor said.

'What are you talking about?'

'There's nothing I can do for him, it's too advanced.'

The words sunk in and hit me like a right hook from Muhammad Ali and I remember thinking that there was obviously some sort of mistake.

'I'm not with you,' I said. 'We are talking about Terry Barry?'

'Yes,' he said, nodding apologetically. 'There's nothing I can do for him... he has testicular cancer and only a few weeks to live. You need to get your affairs in order, Mrs Barry.'

He kept saying this over and over again. Get your affairs in order.

This wasn't happening. This couldn't be true. He had only

just found the lump – surely if he had testicular cancer we had caught it in time, surely there was a cure?

I sat down at the doctor's desk bombarding him with questions, desperately searching for a glimmer of hope, a hint of optimism in the doctor's voice.

'Surely he has some chance of survival?'

'I could be wrong,' he said, 'but I'm 99% sure he has advanced testicular cancer, in which case it will have spread to other parts of his body.'

I burst into tears and ran from the room. Terry was outside standing in the sunshine, looking absolutely stunned.

'So he's told you,' he said. I nodded and threw myself into his arms.

'It can't be true, it can't be true,' I bawled through the tears.

The bus journey home was the longest one I have ever undertaken. We sat in silence most of the way. Terry offered a glimmer of hope as we stepped from the bus. 'I suppose we could always ask for a second opinion...'

'Yes,' I said. 'A second opinion. That would be good.'

I don't think either of us slept for more than an hour that evening. We lay awake talking and mulling things over and the words 'get your affairs in order' tormented me. In those days doctors were seldom wrong; doctors were respected, educated men who studied hard in medical schools for many years. The doctor was a man of many years' experience; surely he had to be almost 100% certain to break news like that to a young couple with a small child.

Normally young Terry slept like a log. He was a good baby, sleeping for eight or nine hours at a time, but for some reason that night he was very restless. I attended to him at least a dozen times and each time my eyes fell on his beautiful little face I burst into tears thinking his days with his father were numbered. This was so unfair; I was a good mother and a good wife and Terry was the nicest man in the world. Surely we didn't deserve this? My son needed his father, he needed his father to take him to the park and run along the beach with him and teach him how to swim and play football and climb trees. This wasn't happening; a son needed a father and a wife needed her husband too.

What had I done wrong? I asked myself. As the early morning light penetrated the curtains and I craved rest and peace. I climbed out of bed and prayed. I begged forgiveness, convincing myself I was somehow to blame. Just what was it I had done to make God punish me this way?

The next few days were a blur. One of the first decisions we took was to move back to Burnley. I don't know why, again it seemed like a good idea at the time. I fought the thought that I was taking Terry back home to die but the feeling was never far away and it came back to haunt me again and again.

Within 24 hours of moving back to Burnley we sought that second opinion. At one point – I can't believe it now – we weren't going to bother, such was the respect and trust we had for our family doctor. We were almost ready to sit down, put our affairs in order and watch Terry slip away. But we did take a second opinion and thank the Lord we did because as a result of the wonderful treatment we received at Christie's Hospital, Terry lived another 36 years.

The first thing that became abundantly clear was how out of order the doctor had been in telling us that the disease was irreversible and terminal. One doctor at Christie's hospital even called him a prat. Don't get me wrong, Terry did have testicular cancer. Our GP had diagnosed that correctly but he had no right to send us out of his surgery with no hope whatsoever and certainly had no authority to tell us that Terry only had weeks to live.

It was Doctor Farmer at Christie's who removed the cancerous testicle almost immediately during an operation and then commenced treatment the very next day. I consoled myself with the thought that there was at least some hope if these wonderful doctors were prepared to operate and at least attempt some sort of treatment. The road would be long and hard, they said to us, and the treatment may not work, but there was a glimmer of a spark of something in the doctor's eyes and I noticed it and I clung to it, daring to believe the impossible.

Immediately they confined Terry to bed for a month and said they would be starting laser treatment which was a cancer treatment that fired a laser beam at the affected area attempting to kill the cancer cells. He received the laser treatment every day at noon for one minute, no more and no less. I remember what the GP said – that it was so advanced that it would have spread to other parts of the body – and yet the hospital were only concentrating on the area near to Terry's groin. He'd got it wrong.

They warned us it wouldn't be very pleasant but although they didn't say so I got the impression it was all that was on offer. There was no other treatment, no alternative. The sickness and diarrhoea were terrible and seemed to last for months, and as a consequence Terry lost nearly three stone in weight.

I remember walking down the hospital corridor trying to take everything in. We'd been told that Terry wouldn't be able to father any more children, which put paid to our hopes of a big family. I was feeling more than a little sorry for myself and burst into tears. A large Afro-Caribbean hospital domestic came over to me and wrapped her arms around me. She told me not to worry. I blurted out that my husband had cancer and she told me to have faith.

'He's in the best place in the world,' she whispered to me. 'They'll save him here.' Then she looked me in the eyes as she wiped a tear or two from my cheeks. 'They'll save him my dear,' she said. 'I promise they will.'

I believed her. I truly believed her and in the course of time she was proved right.

I never ever saw that wonderful lady again though I looked for her on every visit. If by a strange quirk of fate she ends up reading these words in this book I want her to know that she gave me a much-needed boost and I can never thank her enough, nor will I ever forget her beautiful smiling face.

Several months into the treatment the doctor announced that Terry was clear of the disease. We were ecstatic and even though the doctor advised us to exercise a little caution I knew as he uttered those magical words that Terry and I were destined to spend many years together. Terry had to go back to the hospital every three months for a check-up at first, then every six months and then once a year. Eventually they decreased it to every five years and I knew then that we'd finally defeated it.

Even way back in those days I'm not too sure I believed in miracles or divine intervention, but I had my faith and I was convinced that someone was looking over us. In reality Dr Death had made an incredible balls-up.

They say lightning can't strike twice, but believe me it can. Several years later our family was destined to go through exactly the same thing this time with my brother Tommy. He had found a lump in his testicle too, and given what had happened to Terry, he was whisked off to the doctors in double-quick time. The doctor examined him, smiled and said it was nothing to worry about – he had swollen glands. We all breathed a sigh of relief and given our experiences with premature diagnoses, we thought no more about it and waited for the swelling to subside.

But it didn't. Poor Tommy was in considerable pain and started to complain of discomfort in his stomach and his ribs too. Dad took Tommy to the surgery another two or three times and each time the doctor carried out a further examination. Dad described how at one point the doctor sighed and told them he had waiting room full of patients and really had to be getting on with his work. Although Tommy was still in some pain, he and Dad left the surgery reassured that there really was nothing wrong with him and perhaps thinking he was making a little bit more fuss than he ought to. Dad asked if they could have a second opinion but the doctor said there was no need; he instead diagnosed a severe head cold, prescribed some pain killers and sent Tommy home. By this time I was getting really worried and urged Tommy to seek advice from Christie's Hospital.

Dad rang the surgery requesting an appointment via the family GP but it never materialised. In fact, the doctor called Dad up and told him to stop wasting the health service's time; there were sick people in the area, he said, who needed his help and we should really start thinking about them. Several weeks went by and Tommy fought the urge to contact the doctor again, despite the pain getting progressively worse. He was now complaining of pains throughout his body, in his chest and his lower stomach, and a mysterious lump had appeared on his neck. Understandably Tommy refused to go to the doctor's surgery again – he didn't want to waste the doctor's time.

In desperation one evening, with Tommy in agony, Dad telephoned the surgery and asked to be put through to the doctor. The doctor was furious, claiming he'd been disturbed during an important examination with a sick patient. He said he'd had enough and was exercising his right to strike Tommy from his medical panel. In his opinion there was absolutely nothing wrong with Tommy; he was a hypochondriac and he had no intention of ever examining him again. Before Dad had a chance to speak the phone had been slammed down on him. Sure enough, a hand-delivered letter appeared the next day. I can remember reading the doctor's letter as if it was only yesterday. The middle of the letter went something like this:

I have taken the decision to remove you from my medical panel. This is not a decision I have taken lightly nor do I take it often. But as a general practitioner I must protect my patients who are genuinely ill. I can no longer afford to waste my time on people who claim to be sick and who aren't, as time with patients who really need me is very precious.

Tommy was without a GP and Dad started to ring around anywhere and everywhere trying to secure him one. A few days later a Doctor Sahid came out to examine him. Within 20 minutes he had called an ambulance and insisted he went to Christie's Hospital. He was seen within ten minutes. Tommy was asked to strip down to his underwear and underwent an immediate examination. It didn't last too long, confirming what the doctors had suspected simply by looking at him. They took a biopsy to make sure.

Poor Tommy was riddled with cancer; it had spread right through his body and there was nothing they could do for him other than make him pain-free as possible. The doctor in the hospital, Doctor Farmer, asked Dad when the symptoms had first appeared and nearly fell off his seat as Dad described how the first swelling had developed over six weeks earlier. I knew from my experience with Terry that Tommy could have been saved and could have still been alive to this day. The timeframe was almost identical: Terry had gone to the doctor within days of discovering a lump and so had Tommy. The difference in the two doctors' diagnoses was a million miles apart. Terry's doctor gave him weeks to live and Tommy's quack (no apologies for calling him that) said there was nothing wrong with him, and yet they both had testicular cancer. The doctors at Christie's were almost as distraught as we were.

But there was no hope – none whatsoever – and they admitted Tommy to hospital that same day. My poor, beautiful brother wasted away before my very eyes. The medical team wanted to keep him in hospital as that was the best place for him to be. But Tommy didn't want to be there. In the end he begged to come home to die and although the hospital didn't want to let him go, in the end they relented and we took him home.

We all knew he was dying. I don't think it can get any worse than that, watching someone you love dying and not being able to do a single thing about it. I prayed harder than I have ever prayed in my life for some sort of miracle or divine intervention. Mam prayed too, as did Dad, and all of our immediate families, and yet part of me realised that Tommy was beyond hope and there was no way back. Even if a miracle cure had been found overnight his body was beyond repair and Tommy too had resigned himself to the fact that his life was over.

A few days before he died, Tommy gave me a letter. God love him, he wasn't the greatest writer in the world and yet a letter was more powerful than the most meaningful book ever written. He apologised for dying before Christmas because it meant he was unable to give young Terry the present he'd wanted to give him. He gave me some money and told me to buy a present and remind young Terry about his uncle Tommy occasionally. The letter tore my heart and even now I'm finding it very difficult to even write about it.

He weighed no more than six stone in the end. I'd like to say he died peacefully but he didn't; he was racked with pain. Even so, he died where he wanted to die, with his family, in the house that he loved.

He died in my father's arms. I can't quite recall who was at his bedside, a doctor and a nurse I think, and I believe even the priest was there – or so I've been told. All I can remember was Dad's face as he cradled Tommy in his arms while his beloved son slipped away. We all knew at that very moment that Tommy had died and Mam collapsed on the floor sobbing hysterically as someone, though I don't recall who, tried to help her to her feet.

Dad took the original doctor to a tribunal in Manchester citing professional incompetency and negligence. We had the support of the hospital and all of the records of the visits to the doctor's surgery. It seemed fairly clear cut to me, or for any outsider looking in. But as our solicitor said at the time, it would be a difficult one to win. 'You can't pin a doctor down,' was the phrase he used. And sure enough, when the doctor stood in the dock, he refused to admit that he was wrong or that he had made any mistakes. He claimed that Tommy had shown no signs of real discomfort during any of the examinations. Dad was flabbergasted and the records of his numerous phone calls to the surgery weren't even brought up.

We lost. That is to say, the doctor won his right to continue practising medicine. He wasn't found guilty or negligent and went on to practice for many years.

As the hearing finished, Dad made his way outside. The doctor followed him and caught up with him as he reached the door. He admitted that he got it wrong. Dad was furious and I don't know how he never hit him.

'Then why didn't you say that in the court?' asked Dad.

The doctor just shook his head and said it wasn't possible. 'I'm sorry, Mr Blackledge, sincerely sorry.'

Dad pointed outside. 'Burnley Cemetery is just along the road, Doctor,' he said. 'Go and tell my son you're sorry because that's where he's buried.'

Tommy was just 26 years of age.

CHAPTER 11

Unforeseen Circumstances

I took Tommy's death badly. It was so unfair; there was no reason for his death. None whatsoever. Everything I read, everything I watched on television told me the world was filled with horrible evil people and here they were living normal lives, but Tommy was dead. Where was the justice in all this? Tommy never hurt a fly in his entire life; he was a caring and loving person just like Dad and never said a bad word about anybody. So why had God taken him and why had he taken him at such an early age? I could've handled it if Tommy had lived his life, married and had children, achieved what he wanted to achieve. There is something about a young person dying that hits you so much harder.

My husband Terry suffered as a result of Tommy's death in

that his wife was on a distant planet for several months. I wasn't aware of anything from the moment I left the cemetery, even to the point of neglecting my own family. I'd cry uncontrollably at the drop of a hat and Terry would just take me in his arms and hug me until the tears subsided. Terry took over the domestic chores and spent a lot more time with his son. Little things like taking a walk in the park, or jumping on a bus or a train to Blackpool or Morecambe were simply beyond me. Every corner I turned there was something that reminded me of my darling brother's death and I couldn't cope with it. I'd look at people in the news – a paedophile, a scrounger on benefits, a burglar or a mugger – and question why on earth they were still living and Tommy wasn't. I wanted them all dead, every one of them. I wanted them dead and I wanted Tommy back.

Tommy's death was hard to take as we were very close and I think it affected me even more because of what we had been through as a family with Terry's cancer scare. However, I had a young son and of course I needed to get on with my life for his sake.

I cried bucket-loads of tears for poor Tommy but tried to keep my emotions intact in front of young Terry. It was a difficult time. I'd get Terry bathed and ready for bed in his pyjamas and read him a story before tucking him in, and then I'd take myself to the sanctity of my kitchen, sit down with a cup of tea and cry for hours. I asked myself the question 'why?' over and over again – *why us, why Tommy?* We were a nice family; Tommy was a nice lad; why had God taken him at such an early age? I suppose they are questions that all religious people ask themselves when such dramatic events occur.

In desperation I turned to the church and to Father Frar. I suppose I gave him a hard time, too, asking him on many occasions where our God was. Father Frar was sympathetic and kind, and his words soothed and comforted me at times, but of course he never answered my more direct questions, simply stating that God works in mysterious ways.

I read the Madeleine McCann story recently, written by her mother Kate. It was a powerful account of the events leading up to the disappearance of her daughter. Kate too wrestled with her faith; she was also a practising Catholic as I was at the time of Tommy's death. It's hard to accept such an awful thing happening to you, particularly when you have dedicated a fair chunk of your life to God, the church and in particular the Catholic faith. Kate McCann turned to God and begged him to return her beloved daughter safe and sound. She called on her own church back home and all the parishioners and churches in Portugal where her daughter was taken. She called on everybody she knew to pray. She was granted an audience with the Pope and at one point she figured there were millions of people in the world praying for Madeleine. Surely, she thought to herself, with this many people praying something would happen. Sadly Madeleine is still missing and her prayers remain unanswered. Kate McCann wobbled many times, wondering if religion was simply a crutch to lean on when the going got tough. She wondered whether religion was only for the weak and merely an invention of mankind to control the masses. Whatever it is, no one can deny it brought

Kate McCann immense comfort during the initial period of her daughter's disappearance. She battled through with her demons and the dark times, and put all of her doubts to the back of her mind. Whatever your views are on God and his existence you can't help but admire someone like Kate McCann who still to this day retains her faith. I hope that one day that faith is rewarded and her prayers are heard. Reading Kate's book brought everything back to me. I was somehow there with her.

For days, weeks possibly even months after Tommy's death, it was as if I was on automatic pilot – a walking zombie – and there is hardly a week that goes by when I don't think about Tommy, my darling little brother. I still pray for him and I don't think I'll ever get over his death.

And yet, back then, I had to. I had to act normal, be a mother and a wife too. By this time Terry was back at work and was showing no sign of illness whatsoever. Little Terry was now at school and the hours of loneliness were hard to take. I applied for a job in a small café in Burnley Market. It was called Holden's, and I would go on to work there for nearly 20 years. George Holden, the owner, interviewed me – if you could call it that. It was all a bit of a formality. I liked George and he liked me, it was as simple as that. The café was spotlessly clean and I like to think that I turned myself out quite well. He was an ideal employer and I loved every second of my time there. I was in my element – face-to-face with the public for the first time in my working life. When I began to think back, the factories and the mills and even Pontins had lacked close contact with real people. The clientele that ventured into Holden's Café were working-class, honest, ordinary people, just like myself, and I warmed to every one of them. The staff behind the counter were just the same and we worked like one big happy family. The money wasn't good and career prospects almost non-existent, but I was happy and had no intention of looking for another position. I loved the atmosphere of old Burnley Market and the characters that graced the market stalls. Each one had a story to tell and often did so over a plateful of bacon and eggs and a cup of tea.

I was in my mid-20s at the time and I was as happy as I could be with a loving, healthy husband and a beautiful son who was now at school. Tommy's death was still in the forefront of my mind but the constant hustle and bustle of Burnley Market and Holden's Café kept me occupied for most of the day.

People often ask me when my desire to be an actress took hold. Most of them have a misconception that it was something I carried with me from my childhood. It wasn't. I can honestly say that it wasn't ever part of my agenda. I think my working ambition kind of faded away after the disappointment of the WAAF. I was only too pleased that I'd escaped the factories and the mills and, if I'm honest about it, that was the sum total of my ambition or rather the lack of it. As I've said, I was happy and enjoyed my role as a working mother. At times it felt as if there wasn't a spare minute in the day and yet I looked forward to every aspect of it. I looked forward to getting Terry ready for school and then going to the market. I enjoyed my working day and then picking up a few bits and pieces on my way home in preparation for the evening meal.

I daresay my fellow *Shameless* cast, particularly some of the girls, will find that quite surprising; but no, Alice Barry did not have any inclination or long-standing dream to tread the boards or make it onto any sort of screen, be it silver or television. This was the early 1970s and actors and actresses were people who generally came from America. There wasn't even such a thing as daytime television back then, just the BBC in the evenings. We had the cinema, of course, but I can't ever recall sitting in the darkness of the cinema dreaming about being one of the stars of the screen. No, I just sat there and enjoyed the movie and never thought I was the sort of girl who could turn my hand to acting. And besides, *Last Tango in Paris* was doing the rounds then and I mean, what Maria Schneider and Marlon Brando got up to in that film – who would want to be an actress anyway?

I think it must have been about seven or eight years after I started work in Holden's when a new lady came into the café one day. She was very loud and flamboyant and told me that she had just opened a handbag stall. I guess I warmed to her straight away. She was roughly the same height as me with dark, bouffant hair and thick-rimmed gold-framed glasses. I'd like to say she was 'stout' or 'pleasantly plump' but she wasn't, she was fat.

Her name was Thelma Goldberg, a Jewish lady who could talk for England. She had a passion for acting, and whenever her stall was quiet she'd leave her friend in charge and slip away for a cup of tea and talk to me. I confess she was a fascinating lady and whilst other people found her a little boring I absorbed every word she said. At Holden's we had a small serving hatch that looked onto the market, the idea being that the stall holders could nip away from their stalls and place an order at the hatch while keeping an eye on their wares. Thelma was always there with one eye on her stall and one eye on whatever we were making for her. At times I felt positively guilty for the amount of hours I stood at that serving hatch nattering with Thelma about this and that the ways of the world but mostly we talked about acting. I never did discover what major roles Thelma had once played (if any) but she talked a good game and I never tired of listening to her describing her latest work as an extra. Sadly that was the only work she got at that point in her life, but it never seemed to matter to her because she loved just being involved in some way no matter how small. Occasionally she got a speaking part in a drama or a production within the theatre and of course as soon as she received the news she couldn't wait to tell me.

Thelma is long gone now and she always kept her cards a little bit close to her chest but I suspect she never quite made the dizzy heights she aspired to get to. Our industry is notoriously fickle and unemployment is part of the job description, so I wouldn't be surprised if Thelma ended up selling handbags on Burnley Market to make a living. I suspect she was one of tens of thousands who ended up like that and yet she never lost the love for acting and cinema and talking about it.

So if my arm was twisted behind my back and I was

pushed to say who ignited that little spark that propelled me into a career that would last nearly 40 years I would have to say it was Thelma. And who gave me my big break? That would be Thelma too. I can picture the day vividly, as if it was only yesterday. I was standing by the serving hatch looking on to the market. It was a quiet day, the weather grey and miserable. It wasn't raining but it was the sort of day that rain was in the air and each time you looked up into the sky you were convinced the first raindrops were about to fall. I'd spotted Thelma from quite a way off: she was wearing a very colourful dress totally out of tune with the type of day it was. She was walking towards the serving hatch a little quicker than normal with a big grinning smile on her face. She proceeded to tell me that her agency was looking for more extras.

'An extra?' I said, 'What's an extra?' Thelma looked at me as if I was stupid and as if I hadn't been listening to a word she'd been saying for the last six years.

'An *extra*!' she boomed in her big loud voice that carried across the whole of Burnley Market. 'An extra, Alice. The unsung heroes of our industry; the actors and actresses who stand in the background and are occasionally called upon to say a few words on screen.'

I looked at her incredulously. 'Me, an extra? An actress?' I said.

Thelma was nodding, grinning like a Cheshire cat.

'Yes, why not?' she said. 'It's fascinating to go on set and watch and they pay you as well.'

Almost straight away I could picture myself in the role. Mr

Holden was simply the nicest man on earth and I knew that if necessary he would give me the time off and I could make up the hours. My mind was working overtime, I was thinking about what I would say to Terry and how I could get my young son picked up from school. I was daydreaming and envisaging each role while poor Thelma filled me in on the details which of course I wasn't listening to.

Thelma obviously noted the grin that was slowly pulling across my face. And she was smiling too. 'You have to meet my agent Ray, he'll sort everything out for you,' she said.

'Let's have a cup of tea to celebrate,' I said, as Thelma nodded and I went to put the kettle on. Thelma came into the café and sat by the seat next to a payphone. As I placed her cup of tea on the counter next to her she was already making a phone call to her agent.

Thelma made an appointment for me. Ray lived in Manchester which to me seemed like a million miles away. Immediately I began to get cold feet but Thelma talked me round. The dastardly deed was done and I was to meet with Ray after work the following day. *Why was I so bloody nervous?* I thought – I was only going for an audition as an extra! I smashed three or four cups and plates that day and I was convinced at one point Mr Holden might even sack me. God love him, he didn't; in fact he sent me home an hour earlier so I could prepare myself. That was typical of Mr Holden – one of the nicest men I have ever met.

Ray lived in a large house on the outskirts of the city centre. I think it was in Didsbury but I may be wrong, it was such a long time ago. I remember walking up a long gravel driveway to a large open door that led to the entrance hall. I was so nervous you'd think I was attending the audition for a place on *Gone With The Wind*! Any delusions of grandeur, however, were shattered in an instant as Ray came to the door smoking a cigarette and holding a half-finished cup of tea. He was nice and friendly but I expected a little more glamour. He invited me in and we sat at his kitchen table where he proceeded to make me a cup of tea too. The one-page 'contract' sat on the kitchen table already prepared. Ray chatted about the weather and how Manchester United were doing and anything else he could think of, but he didn't ask about my acting experience or what I'd done in the past. I was a 'face', and one he obviously liked because he pushed the contract across the table almost immediately. I signed it and then it was over. I had got the gig (as we actresses say!)

Ray did warn me that extra work wasn't something that I should rely on but I reminded him that I worked on Burnley Market and that's how I knew Thelma. I told him I would be grateful for anything that came along and that I wasn't really interested in the money side of things – it was more for the experience and being able to see the television and film profession first hand. I have to admit at this point that I was not interested in becoming an actress. I wanted and expected to go no further than being a background extra. I suppose Thelma had ignited something during her many lectures and yes, I wanted to see how a real film set worked and this was my big opportunity. But I wanted nothing more. I asked Ray what sort of work he expected to get me. He shrugged his shoulders and said 'Who knows? It could be anything and it could be nothing.' He told me it was more likely to be in advertising although it could be just about anything – television, film, occasionally even the theatre.

I was mesmerised. He had triggered something inside me and I was tingling all over. I never, ever expected that I would even be talking about film and television let alone discussing my participation. I travelled back home in a daze and even missed my stop and had to walk back in the rain. I couldn't wait to tell Terry but he was less than interested as he ate his evening meal and listened to me talk for England.

A few days later I remember watching an episode of *Coronation Street*. I was no longer watching it from the perspective of an average television viewer. No, not me. I was now analysing every frame and being critical of the director's angles and even the actors. I was also studying every single person in the background of each set. How sad was that? I'd never even set foot on the stage or on a film set and yet overnight I'd become Alfred Hitchcock!

It was about two weeks before the first letter came from Ray's agency. I thought it would say he'd changed his mind – a 'don't call us, we'll call you' type of letter. But I was wrong. On the third line down it clearly stated I'd been allocated a little extra work – two weeks to be exact. And the next line nearly blew me away. *Oh no!* (or should that be 'oh yes'?) I was being put forward for a part in *Coronation Street*! I read the letter again, shaking like a leaf. I'd made it, I'd reached the dizzy heights of the silver screen. I was going to be an extra in the Rovers Return!

And the money was fantastic. Ray was quoting a figure

of £70 per day. I think his expenses and commissions came off that final figure but all the food and drink was included and all I had to find was the bus fare to Manchester and back.

I was in my element and couldn't wait to tell Terry. At least this time he was a little bit more interested. *Coronation Street* was on television again that evening. Young Terry couldn't understand why I had him bathed and ready for bed by six o'clock but there was no way he going to disturb my night in front of the telly. I plonked myself down on the sofa at least an hour beforehand with a packet of liquorice allsorts to chew on (after all I needed to concentrate!) It's quite an art sitting at a bar table nursing a glass of non-alcoholic wine. Not something that everyone can turn their hand to and I had to take notes.

Coronation Street was everything I expected it to be; I was simply fascinated and even the big stars all had a friendly word or two for the dozens of extras who worked with them. Off screen was a little tedious, I must admit, as we all sat around waiting for something to happen. We weren't allowed on the set if we weren't required and we were all confined to a large but comfortable room. There were tea and coffee making facilities and a radio, but most of the extras just chatted amongst themselves or read a book. I soon discovered there was an art to being an extra: you have to have patience. I can remember some days when I turned up at seven o'clock in the morning and waited in the room for 12 hours, only to be told I wasn't required. That was heart-breaking and soul destroying, but then again we were well fed and I was making money. That was what Terry told me when I started moaning to him on such days.

One of the director's assistants would appear in the doorway and read the names of the extras required for that particular set. It was music to my ears when she called out my name. 'Alice Barry required on set,' she would say. It has a certain ring to it, don't you think?

And then I was in my element. The same assistant would point me in the right direction and get me into position. She had a little diagram with everybody's positions drawn on it and of course they all had to be exactly the same as the previous shoot. Nothing was left to chance and I remember there was even a young girl whose sole occupation was to draw the footsteps of the main characters on the floor of the Rovers Return. In one scene I was standing at the bar and I had my very own set of footprints. How good is that?

I was hooked on the television industry. I could have quite easily forgone the waiting around and the 'green room' but once I was on set I loved it and the time flew by. And I couldn't quite describe to you, my dear reader, what it was like that first night as I sat by the television with my gorgeous husband and waited for my first appearance on *Coronation Street*.

You can trawl the old videotapes as much as you want, I guarantee you won't see me. My appearance was brief to say the least, all of about two seconds, and even then the main camera was focused on the actors involved in the scene while Alice Barry was a soft hazy blur in the background. Nevertheless it was an exciting moment and Terry and I squealed for joy as we spotted me, the would-be superstar. We had such a laugh as I explained that I had waited around all day for that two-second moment. When you next watch a big production or even just *Coronation Street* on a wet Wednesday night spare a little thought for the extras; as Thelma said they really are the unsung heroes of every motion picture, every television programme or series ever made. I have a great rapport with the extras on *Shameless*. That's because I've been there, done it, got the t-shirt, and I know exactly what they go through day by day.

Over the years I appeared in *Coronation Street* several times as an extra and of course in a few speaking roles too. I remember turning up on set one day and being put immediately onto a bus. We were told that we were heading for Yorkshire – Thirsk to be exact. We were filming a scene in a real prison next to Thirsk racecourse. When we entered the prison we all had to be frisked as if we were real visitors. We extras played the part of visitors sitting at the tables while a scene was played out.

The first year with Ray's agency was magical and I had work almost every month. I appeared in *Emmerdale Farm* (as it was then) too and auditioned as an extra for a television series based around the Yorkshire Ripper. I didn't get that part which was a little disappointing as criminology interests me greatly and I was really looking forward to getting my teeth into that one. I suppose I wasn't quite glamorous enough for what they were looking for. Perhaps they wanted me to play the part of a prostitute and I just didn't have what it took. Thank God for that!

Even as an extra you really get your teeth into a role and become the character the director wants you to be. It doesn't matter whether you have a speaking role or not, every extra wants to do their best just in case one person out of the millions of viewers casts a roving eye in their direction. I remember one scene we were filming for *Coronation Street*. It took place in a Manchester nightclub called Foo Foo Lamarr's. The nightclub had a reputation for attracting drag queens from Manchester's gay community and over the top dressed-up females who feel more than comfortable dancing the night away in that type of place. The downside was that we had to start filming once the nightclub was closed shortly after three in the morning. The wardrobe department of *Coronation Street* went to town that day and gave us some crazy outfits. I wore a short red leather miniskirt with fishnet stockings and a low-cut blouse. The extras met up on a bus that was to take us to the nightclub. What a laugh we had; everyone looked ridiculous but as usual we slipped into the role just perfectly. In fact we must've been bloody good because after we left the nightclub when we'd wrapped it was round about seven o'clock in the morning. The only people on the street were the bin men and street cleaners and a postman or two. We paraded past one of the council bin wagons and the poor lads on board were convinced we were the real thing. Did they give us some abuse, and I can tell you it wasn't very pleasant either. They called us tarts and slags and gave us rather offensive hand gestures. Whereas the real ladies of the night were hardened to that sort of thing and would have likely gave as good as they got, we were shocked and petrified. We hung our heads in shame and ran like hell for the bus. It was all a big joke of course, and it was a good story to share with our husbands when we got home. If we could fool the average man on the street then we were all good actresses!

CHAPTER 12

A Brief Introduction to Acting

As the years passed by my life seemed to settle down and I fell into three distinct roles. I was a wife and mother, a waitress at Holden's Café and an extra whenever Mr Holden granted me the time off (which was quite often). In fact I can't remember any occasion where Mr Holden wouldn't allow me time away from the café; even during the holidays he was more than happy to put in a few extra hours himself and ask favours of the staff in realigning their hours. I owe much to my dear friends at Holden's Café and hopefully I made them aware of just how much at the time.

From a financial point of view things were looking up. Terry was showing no ill effects from the cancer and was working full-time. With my wages from Holden's Café and the higher paid extra work which was becoming quite regular we found ourselves in the envious position of dreaming about a foreign holiday. This was not a common occurrence back then – at least not in the working-class communities where we lived. Terry and I decided on Majorca; it wasn't too far away and just about within our price bracket. I remember our son Terry had just moved away from home and it would be our first holiday without him. Neither of us had flown before and we were really excited as we boarded the plane at Manchester airport.

I wasn't frightened nor was I apprehensive; it was the curiosity that had me sitting on the edge of my seat fidgeting like a little schoolgirl at Christmas time. Terry kept nudging me and asking what was wrong. I just kept repeating over and over again, 'not long now.' Terry thought I was talking about landing in Majorca.

I wasn't and I waited patiently.

We were above the clouds and the pilot announced that we had reached our cruising altitude. This was as high as the aeroplane would go and I began looking out the window. I was straining to get a better look, squashing myself deeper and deeper into the seat to get the maximum angle to look even higher up into the sky. It was then that Terry nudged me.

'What are you looking for, Alice? There's nothing up there but sky. Just what is it you are expecting to see?'

I sat upright in my seat and looked at him as if he was daft.

'Heaven,' I said

'What?'

'I'm looking for Heaven – I can't see it. Surely it must be out there somewhere?'

Terry started laughing. 'You cannot be serious?' he said. 'You're looking for *Heaven*?'

'Yes.'

He lifted my glass from the fold-away tray in front of me. 'I think you've had one too many brandies, Alice, time to switch to lemonade.'

Looking back on that incident I feel so naïve and rather silly, and part of me didn't want to share that experience with you. But honestly, I really did expect to see Heaven that day; I expected to see the pearly gates, clouds with angels on, bright stars and fairy lights, and I expected to see long-departed members of my family including Tommy. I hadn't thought it through, of course – how could every single deceased person in the entire world be standing on a few clouds in a convenient position where my aircraft would just happen to fly past?

But I really did believe that I would see Heaven that day and I was so disappointed, even though my husband thought it was just about the funniest joke of the year.

Oh no, I knew I shouldn't have put that in. David Threlfall will have a field day when I'm next on set!

As the years rolled by my son became a father himself. Doesn't time fly? Young Shaun, my first grandchild – and Mam and Dad's first great-grandchild – was born on 13 September 1986. My wonderful parents worshipped the ground he walked on and we were never out of each other's company for too long. We shared meals together, walks along the canal and day trips to Morecambe and Blackpool. The weekend of Shaun's first birthday we decided to take the train to Morecambe. Terry (my son Terry) was working which was a little unfortunate but nevertheless Shaun's grandparents and great-grandparents were determined to make a day of it – a kind of celebration. It was a beautiful day and I remember being quite excited as mam pushed the pram and I walked between my husband and my father along the busy promenade.

We stopped at one of those little shops that sell buckets and spades, beach balls and swimming costumes. We bought Shaun a little red bucket and spade and a little bit further along there was a baker's shop where we bought some pasties, sausage rolls and teas in polystyrene cups. We'd brought towels from home and I'd packed a little umbrella which fixed onto the pram to shade Shaun from the sun. It was a perfect day with perfect company – my wonderful caring parents, my gorgeous husband and my perfect little grandson – and we made our way to the beach.

Nothing could possibly go wrong.

As we walked towards the beach I remember Dad hesitating. He appeared to be looking around for a seat on the promenade.

'C'mon Dad,' I said. 'Let's find a spot on the beach.'

Dad found a space on a wooden bench and said he was happy to sit there. I wouldn't have it. We were on Morecambe beach and we had a bucket and spade so we were playing in the sand – everybody, Mam, Dad, me, Terry and Shaun.

Dad was shaking his head insisting on staying put.

'Leave your dad where he is,' Mam said, 'he'll be quite happy there watching us.'

I wouldn't have it.

We'd come all the way to Morecambe beach and I was insistent that we were all going onto the sand. As Mam and Terry were lifting the pram onto the beach, Mam told me I was wasting my time. 'Your father doesn't like the sand,' she said.

I shouted to Mam and Terry to walk on ahead and sat on the seat next to my dad. He was looking a little anxious.

'What's wrong, Dad?' I asked. 'Don't you like the sand between your toes?' I pointed to young Shaun. 'That's your first great-grandson,' I said, 'and he wants his great-grandad to play sandcastles with him.'

'You go on ahead, Alice,' he said, 'and I'll stay here if you don't mind.'

But I did mind.

I was beginning to lose my temper. What was wrong with him and why was he trying to spoil my day? It was one of those occasions that don't come along too often and it was made worse as I noticed other grandparents playing in the sand with their grandchildren. Was it really too much to ask why Dad was being so stubborn?

And then he spoke. 'I don't like beaches, Alice. I haven't set foot on a beach for 45 years.'

He pointed to the beach. 'You see buckets and spades and clear blue sea, sandcastles and picnic rugs.' Dad was shaking his head. 'Not me. I see broken bodies, men lying face down in the sand and severed arms and legs and pieces of shrapnel, and the sea as red as a pillar box and I don't want to go there. I'm sorry, Alice, I just don't want to go there.'

I was speechless, absolutely horrified. Dad was back in Dunkirk reliving the torment and the agony of World War Two. I couldn't quite believe it. Was it really 45 years since he'd set foot on a beach?

I sat with him for about 15 minutes and talked to him, gently trying to reassure him. As I talked his anxiety seem to subside a little and much to my surprise I persuaded him to set foot on the golden sands of Morecambe Bay. He took his shoes off and sat down on the rug with his great-grandson and made a token attempt to build a sandcastle, though I knew in his heart wasn't in it. He stayed there for about ten minutes and then made an excuse that the sand was cold. He made his way back to the same seat and plonked his backside down with a strange satisfied smile on his face. It was a major achievement for him and I'm glad I helped him overcome his fear. I can't ever recall another visit to a beach with Dad but I'd like to think he managed it at least once or twice without me.

That incident gave me an incredible insight into what war is all about and to this day the thought of another world war terrifies me.

Mam and Dad died within six months of each other. Mam was first to go, never recovering from an angina attack. It's sad but fair to say that Mam was never the same after her accident at the mill. Whilst her mental health was undoubtedly a result of the accident, physically she went downhill almost immediately too. When I saw what the accident had done to Mam I never expected her to live to a great age and I think Tommy's death took years off her life too. I remember thinking her compensation sum was like winning the pools back then; it bought a house, after all. However, looking back and seeing her health and quality of life deteriorate since that fateful day, she should have received millions.

Dad was like a lost soul. I lived next door to him at the time and in the back yard we had an adjoining gate that was always left open. In fine weather he'd sit in the yard and stare into space but I'd always be there for him when I wasn't working. My husband Terry would always look out for him and Terry Junior always had plenty of time for his grandad.

I awoke one day with an enormous sense of dread as if I knew something bad was about to happen. I wasn't working that day and neither was Terry. I bit his head off several times that morning for no particular reason, convinced someone or something was about to do me a bad deed. Nothing went right that day. I broke a glass, burned a cake in the oven and just knew my day was heading from bad to worse. I thought the final straw had come when my washing line broke in the back yard, propelling a line full of washing onto the damp dirty concrete. I cried out, cursing and swearing, unaware Dad could hear me from the open kitchen door. He wandered through the gate.

'What's up, girl?' he said. 'Things can't be that bad that you've to curse like an Irish navvy.'

I was crying, picking my washing up from the floor, moaning that I was the unluckiest girl in the world and that I'd have to start my washing all over again.

'And where am I going to hang the bloody washing?' I said. 'Look at this.' I showed him the broken washing line. 'I knew this would happen, I knew something like this would happen from the minute I woke this morning.'

Dad told me not to fret, said I was being stupid and that he was sure he had a spare one in his cupboard in the kitchen. He helped me pick up the dirty washing, then he disappeared into the kitchen. A few minutes later he appeared with a new line, a pair of pliers and some stepladders. He told me I would have a new clothes line long before the washing was finished.

I came back out into the yard after about 20 minutes and remember being a little puzzled that the new washing line was still lying on the ground. That's when I saw Dad slumped in the corner. I screamed for Terry as I ran over to him. He was still alive but breathing very slowly. Terry ran next door to call for an ambulance and they were there in a matter of minutes. Dad lay in my arms and I cradled his head on my chest. The ambulance men worked on him quickly as I held his hand but then I became aware of a sudden change in him. I can't explain it but I just knew he'd gone. I looked at one of the ambulance men and he confirmed my worst fears.

'I'm sorry, love, he's gone,' he said. 'There's nothing we can do for him.'

Dad was 73.

It was the year 2000 and although I had been in regular extra work for some ten years I still didn't consider myself an actress. If anyone questioned me on my profession outside Holden's Café I would've said 'I do some extra work'. I wasn't an actress, I was an extra. But things were about to change.

I auditioned for the part in the television drama *Cops*. Funnily enough it was playing the part of a café owner. At the time I was thinking of quitting Holden's Café because Mr Holden had sold the café to a new owner. Terry and Marina Burrell were really nice but Mr and Mrs Holden were like family to me and working there without them had lost its appeal.

I went to Bolton for the audition. I say 'audition' but it was hardly like an audition. There were three chairs: one for me, one for the director and one for the producer and they interviewed me. It was like a proper job interview (or so I'd imagine). Whatever I said to them worked, because I got the job. The money was more than generous and I made my mind up; I was quitting the café.

Peggy Hargreaves in *Clocking Off*, *Peter Kay's Phoenix Nights*, *Bob & Rose*, *Coronation Street*, *New Street Law*...the parts came thick and fast and I was never out of work. I'm glad about that because it meant I was always kept busy and that made me just about able to cope with my wonderful parents' deaths.

I received a letter through the post asking me if I wanted to audition for a part in a TV film called *Vacuuming Completely Nude In Paradise*. It was to be directed by

Danny Boyle – bloody hell! And the star of the show was Timothy Spall. My God, *Danny Boyle*. The man was a legend, directing the smash hit *Trainspotting* and a good, Catholic, Lancashire lad. And to put the icing on the cake Terry was a huge fan of Timothy Spall – particularly as the gormless Barry in his favourite programme *Auf Wiedersehen Pet*.

I milked the letter a little as I stood in the kitchen reading it as Terry ate breakfast.

'Well there's a thing, they want me to star in a film with Timothy Spall.'

The mere mention of the man's name had Terry spluttering in his teacup.

'Yeah, it says here.' I showed him the letter and as if by magic his eyes were drawn to the exact line where Timothy Spall's name appeared.

'Don't get excited,' I told him, 'it's only an audition, I'm not guaranteed to get the part.'

But he was excited – this was his hero after all.

The auditions were to be held in Manchester and conveniently Terry was off work after a recent operation. For once he couldn't refuse to come to an audition with me. He had no excuse and there was just a slight chance he might even meet Mr Spall himself.

I've used this expression in the book a couple of times previously but it's the only way I can think of describing Terry as he walked into the studio: he was like a big bloody kid at Christmas time – a nervous wreck, wondering if he'd been good enough to get his stocking filled. I had to laugh.

We both sat down in the waiting room and Terry had a copy of that day's paper which he held open trying to convince everyone that he was actually reading the words and studying the pictures. He wasn't; his eyes and ears were all over the place, trying to get a glimpse of his hero. Every door that opened, every person that walked through the room, every voice that carried from a distant area Terry latched on to.

After ten minutes Bev Keogh, the casting agent, walked into the room. 'Hi Alice,' she said. 'How are you?' I'd worked with Bev before and knew her well and stood up to greet her. She showed me through the door and was just about to point me in the direction of the auditions when she stopped.

'Who's that through there?' She pointed at Terry.

I looked back, thinking that someone else had walked into the room. Terry sat on his own.

'Him?' I said pointing to Terry

'Yes, the chap with the grey hair.'

'Oh, him? Don't mind him, that's my husband Terry and he's just come along to keep me company.'

I was explaining that he was on the sick after his operation but Bev didn't seem to be listening. She just kept muttering 'perfect' over and over again.

'What's perfect, who's perfect?' I asked her.

'Him,' she replied. 'He is perfect to play the part of your husband.'

I burst out laughing and told her to think again; I was going for an audition, I hadn't got the part yet.

'But I know you, Alice, and you're perfect for the part.'

'And yes, Bev, you may be right, but you are a casting agent and it's not your decision.'

'But you look perfect together, a perfect husband-and-wife combination.'

'That's because we are, Beverley!' I laughed.

Bev Keogh was adamant that Terry and I were the perfect couple for the part but I don't know how she persuaded me to go and talk him into it. You can imagine his reaction: he was nervous enough just sitting in the waiting room, there was no way on God's earth anyone was going to persuade him to audition for a part in a movie, particularly when his hero had been cast in the starring role.

I left Bev talking to Terry. I wanted to tell her it was a lost cause and she was wasting her time but she sat with him and shooed me away to my audition.

Danny Boyle held the audition and seemed very down-to-earth, which is perhaps why he brings out the best in the actors and actresses he works with. We went through the rigmarole and I read from the script I had prepared. Danny seemed quite content after I finished and sat back on his seat with his hands on his knees. He gave me a big smile.

'Well Alice, what normally happens now is I send you home and in a week or two you will receive an envelope in the post telling you whether you been successful or not.'

I nodded my head

He continued. 'That's what normally happens but today isn't normal because I'm telling you you've got the part.'

I was flabbergasted.

'I don't need to see anybody else – you have been cast into the role and the job is yours. I like you Alice because you act with your eyes.'

And who are we to argue with Mr *Slumdog Millionaire*? If he liked actresses who act with their eyes then it was good enough for me!

I couldn't wait to get back through to tell Terry. I was in for a big shock, though, because when I returned to the waiting area Bev stood with her arm linked through Terry's and she beamed as she told me that he had agreed to give it a shot.

'My Terry, an actor?' I said. 'You're taking the mickey.'

She wasn't.

I still can't believe to this day that Terry got the part, but he did. During the audition and the eventual filming they somehow managed to make him feel at ease and he played his part well. It was an enormous thrill for Terry just meeting Timothy Spall, and my God, seeing him act in the same scene as Timothy – well that was just about the best thing that could ever have happened to him.

I told Timothy all about Terry's infatuation with him and his favourite programme *Auf Wiedersehen Pet*. He was great and made Terry feel at home and comfortable on every take, but made a point of telling Terry one day that *Auf Wiedersehen Pet* wasn't the only thing he'd ever done. It's true, of course, and I think Timothy is probably a little fed-up of everyone bringing that programme up as it was so long ago (1983), but he was brilliant in it and I suppose it's not unfair to say it gave him his big break. Timothy, if you ever read this book, stand tall and be proud of 'Barry Taylor' because you played a genius role!

Terry was in his element on set and he enjoyed every minute of it. The money was a bonus too. We filmed for about three or four days and the pay was the equivalent to about two months wages at the time. Terry didn't have quite as big a part as I did but his wage was only a few pounds behind me. But that was insignificant to Terry; he was on the sick and was therefore getting paid anyway, so if the production company had pushed a contract in front of him telling him he'd be on two farthings a day he still would have signed it.

It was an incredible experience acting on the same set as your husband with one of the biggest stars in television and the memories of those three or four days are still with me today. It was the first time I've worked with Terry and we both enjoyed every minute. I still have the DVD in my house today and pop it on occasionally. It's rather a surreal experience watching your dead husband on screen, and even more so when you are there with him; however, I do still enjoy watching it and while you might think this is a little sad, when I watch it is generally with something a little alcoholic and a small box of chocolates, and I feel we are together once again – if only for 76 glorious minutes. I always shed a few tears – of course I do – but they are tears of happiness, reliving the wonderful memories I shared for so many years with my big gentle giant.

I would be destined to act with Timothy Spall again in *The Fattest Man In Britain* in 2009 and of course with my good friend Bobby Ball.

CHAPTER 13

Shameless: The Beginning

I've already touched on my decision to take the part in *Shameless* but I will go into it in a little more detail here as I think it's quite important. I had a nice feeling about the show even from the beginning, although initially I was offered a very small part.

My agent called me and asked if I wanted to audition for a part in a new comedy drama called *Shameless*. He explained the format of the show, which at the time seemed quite unique. I readily agreed to the audition and turned up some 30 minutes early. The show's producer, Paul Abbott, was overseeing the auditions, which was a little result in itself because Paul Abbott was from Burnley. Although I didn't know Paul personally I knew some of his sisters and some of his immediate family and thus felt quite comfortable as I walked into the room. I have an incredible admiration for Paul nowadays having gotten to know him a little more. It's fair to say he had a rather stormy childhood and to achieve what he has achieved is nothing short of miraculous. I'm not going to go into too much detail but suggest the curious reader may want to look up Paul on Wikipedia.

Paul sat me down and explained the part I would be auditioning for. I mentioned that I knew some of his family back in Burnley and felt on home ground. 'So you knew me before you got here?' he said.

'Yes.' I replied. 'But I'm a little disappointed because I was told that Jimmy McGovern was holding the auditions!'

That's me, I'm afraid… always putting my mouth into gear before engaging my brain. Jimmy McGovern of Robbie Coltrane's *Cracker* fame (and *Brookside*) is one of my all-time favourite scriptwriters, but at the same time Paul Abbott was very well respected as a writer and a producer too. He had been nominated for six BAFTAs winning two, won Press Guild Awards, Royal Television Society awards, the Writers' Guild of Great Britain and even an Emmy, and yet I was disappointed. I'm a real mug sometimes aren't I?

Paul just laughed it off. It was a good start, a nice icebreaker. Paul said I would be playing the part of a nun, wimple and all. Fantastic, I thought – Father Livey will be pleased. At last I'm going to be a nun, even if in spirit only.

However as he walked onto set with me he explained the role I would be playing. My character, the nun, would walk along to the local shop carrying a basket, but as she approached the doorway of the shop the owner would suddenly appear, close the door and turn the sign to 'closed'. I would mutter a little, turn around, and walk back in the direction I had come from. Some time later, I'd walk towards the shop again and lo and behold the same thing would happen. But the third time would be a bit different. Paul explained what it was he was looking for: on the third occasion I was to peer through the shop window, convinced that the owner was somewhere in the shop laughing his head off. I would then turn around to see if anybody was looking and then face the shop door again. I would punch the door as hard as I could and shout at the top of my voice 'You fucking bastard!'

I'd then turn away from the shop, smooth down my wimple and compose myself. When we did the audition, I noticed that the people watching were all in stitches. Paul, meanwhile, walked over and said it was brilliant.

'It wasn't that good,' I said.

'It was. It was first class,' he said; 'just what I was looking for.'

As I sat on the train on the way home I thanked God that Father Livey hadn't been watching. Good grief, what would he have made of the cursing nun played by one of his faithful!

A few days later I had another phone call from the studio and they told me that Paul wanted to see me again. A good sign, I thought; studios don't normally want to see you just to tell you that you've been unsuccessful. So I walked through and immediately Paul told me he had been thoroughly impressed with my audition.

'But unfortunately we're not going offer you the part,' he said.

The bastard, I thought, dragging me all the way down here to tell me that.

Before I could react he continued.

'I want you to come in as a character called Lillian. It's a far bigger part and it should continue as long as the series continues. The nun was just a bit-part and it's not for you.'

Brilliant, I thought – he obviously liked me. Paul explained the character of Lillian: she was a seamstress, a little bit down on her luck, and I warmed to her immediately. I sat back in my seat as pleased as punch. I'd made it, I thought; I'd made it into *Shameless*.

The contract was for a year which is music to the ears of any actress – but was sure I recalled Paul saying that Lillian would be there for as long as *Shameless* ran. Don't ask me how I knew but I somehow sensed that this project was going to be long-term.

I was excited and feeling quite pleased with myself as I whistled a tune while I cleaned Father Livey's church on a sunny morning in the spring of 2003.

Cleaning the church was part of the unpaid duties I undertook every week. It was quite normal and expected of you as a member of the congregation. There were three or four cleaners made up from the congregation and I remember one man used to maintain the small garden at the side of the church and another lady who used to prepare the flowers every Sunday. None of us ever received any wages or expenses. It would have been almost disrespectful to ask for any money in return. The money the church saved would be better utilised elsewhere, helping the poor and starving in other parts of the world. I daresay it has been going on for centuries.

All I remember is a conversation with Father Livey: a conversation that, if I had listened to him, would have changed my life for the worse. *Shameless* has given me financial stability and of course many wonderful friends who I now look on as a big extended family. I remember I was dusting the tops of the front row of pews in the church, whistling a happy tune, when Father Livey breezed through a side door striding purposely towards me. He wore the full black cassock with the white dog collar and even then (as it does now) it made me draw breath and my heart began to beat just that little bit faster.

'Good morning Alice,' he boomed in that deep powerful voice of his. 'And how are you today?'

'I'm fine,' I answered. And immediately I proceeded to tell him my exciting news. He was instantly on the defensive as if he was searching for something to disapprove of, which was the reaction I was expecting to hear. It was good news to me, of course, and a regular income, all too rare in the profession of acting. As he questioned me as to the content of the show I felt as if I was being deflated. He wasn't smiling and he wasn't pleased for me. I smiled as I mentioned the audition and my role as a nun. He mellowed a little but I put my foot in it as I said she wasn't the normal run of the mill type of nun but a little naughty! Why on earth did I say that?

'Naughty, Alice? In what way?'

I hesitated and stuttered. 'Well, Father...she swears.'

'Swears?'

'Oh don't worry, Father, I didn't get the part – they gave me another part instead.'

But by now the questions were flying at me thick and fast and the more I opened my mouth the bigger the hole I dug for myself. It was an adult television show. I had been told that from the beginning, so what was stopping me telling Father Livey just that? Adult storylines, adult humour, the normal day-to-day happenings that occur on a daily basis on inner-city council estates where the majority of residents live on benefits.

Eventually he forced my hand.

'It's not a children's show, Father Livey.' I said. 'It's aimed at adults and will go out after the watershed.'

'But swearing, Alice?'

'Er...yes Father.'

'Not the "F" word?'

'More than likely.'

Yes, 'fucking' and 'bastard' and 'shit' and 'twat' and even the dreaded 'c**t' too, I should have said. But being a good Catholic I saved Father Livey's embarrassment.

Father Livey still went off on one. At one point I thought he was the one that was going to start using the 'f' word. 'It's the devil's work,' he kept repeating again and again, 'I forbid you to take the role.'

Something happened to me in that short period of time when I stood and fought my corner in the gloom of St Augustine's. Had I seen the light? I don't know, but something definitely changed in me. A man stood before me. No more than that. Father Livey wasn't a saint, he wasn't God. I respected him for what he was – a man of the cloth, a man who had dedicated his life to an organisation. But although he ranted on as if he owned me, as if he was my boss, the harsh reality was that he didn't control me and he had no right to demand anything of me.

Looking back on the incident now I wish I had been a little more forceful or a little stronger, given him a piece of my mind and told him that he had no right to speak to me the way he had. I didn't. I simply hung my duster on the back of the pew and told him I was taking the job. It was my livelihood and I had a family to support and unless the Catholic Church was willing to replace my lost income then they had no right to even offer an opinion.

He was still ranting as I walked out of the building.

Thank God (sorry about the pun) I didn't listen to him, but how many would have done so in that situation? How many frightened individuals would have simply doffed their caps and bowed down to what the priest demanded? I take an altogether different view on religion these days. By all means live and let live, and if you have a faith may you take great comfort from it – I envy you. But don't let it control your life or obsess you, and whatever you do don't force your Gospels or your opinions on other people.

I have been asked many times: was there a point in the conversation where you considered Father Livey's advice? Did you waver at all? I suppose I did. At the beginning of the conversation I felt awkward, like a school girl in front of the headmaster and of course the line of least resistance was to do as he said. But I didn't, I grew stronger. And as I walked back home I analysed the situation from start to finish and wondered to myself if I had in fact made a mistake and did I want to go back and tell Father Livey I had changed my mind? But no, whatever way I looked at it I was happy with my decision, my stance against Father Livey. I confess I was scared and it took me some weeks before I attended mass, but when I did I held my head up high. Father Livey never mentioned our conversation again.

CHAPTER 14

Shameless: Continued

B eing on the set of *Shameless* during those first few weeks reinforced my opinion that I had made the right decision. From the first few hours it was like being at home.

I met up with some old friends, people I'd worked with in the past. Jack Deam was there playing the part of Marty Fisher, a character suffering from Tourette's. I'd worked with Jack on *Clocking Off*; he is a very talented boy and I confess here and now that his portrayal of Marty Fisher is nothing short of genius. James McAvoy was there too, playing Steve McBride. I worked with James for the first two series and it was clear he had an incredible talent. What he has gone on to achieve is no surprise to me and I enjoy watching his career blossom year on year. He was especially good as the doctor in *The Last King of Scotland*. I think it's fair to say

Shameless gave him his big break and I'd like to think he learned a lot on the series working with some very talented individuals like Jack – oh yeah, and a certain Mr Threlfall.

I was in awe of David, who plays the main character, Frank Gallagher. I'd followed his career for some time and yes, I was a great fan and here I was measuring his inside leg in my first scene. I was about to tickle the bollocks of the man who'd played Edgar in *King Lear* opposite a certain Sir Laurence Olivier and Smike in Charles Dickens' *Nicholas Nickleby*... Bloody hell!

My character was Lillian, a down-and-out seamstress. She really was a little bit of a pathetic character and the make-up department went to town on me. They streaked my hair grey and dressed me in a tatty white cardigan and tights. They painted red lines on my face, threw dust at me to make me look really scruffy and then eventually gave me the trademark glasses, by which time Lillian was born. We were in the Gallaghers' house as Frank stood on the coffee table smoking a fag and holding a can of beer. He was being measured for a suit for his daughter's wedding and I had to take his inside leg measurement. The director told me to go for it, 'Get the tape measure and get your hand right up there,' he said, 'get it right up there'. So I did.

They took several shots from different angles. James was laughing and so was David. I think David sensed a little nervousness as I was new on set (I came in a few weeks after the series started). Perhaps I didn't go for it quite as much as the director wanted. Or perhaps I didn't want the moment to end. Either way, for some reason we needed to play the scene over and over again. Eventually we got it right. Afterwards David said, 'Alice, go for it love, my wife's been on holiday for a fortnight!'

In between takes James McAvoy jumped over the coffee table and said 'Alice, I've been dying to meet you, can we have a photograph?' Can you imagine it, James McAvoy asking me for a photograph?

From the very first scene it never ceased to be great fun. David in particular winds me up, teasing me and cracking jokes on and off screen.

My character Lillian started to prosper and go up in the world. They dressed me a little better and I persuaded make-up to get rid of those horrible veins. The directors agreed. Lillian was on the up and up and the veins could go.

I think it's a good time to point out to you, my dear reader, that before I started *Shameless* I never ever swore. I mean *never*. I've already said that I simply loathe the 'c' word but from the first few scenes it was clear to me that I'd entered a world that was quite alien to me. Every other sentence uttered on set had an 'f' at the beginning and even Lillian wasn't averse to the odd curse. It was never a car but a '*fucking* car', the pub was the '*fucking* pub' and every character who graced the streets of the make believe Chatsworth estate was a 'c**t' or a 'twat'.

It was a different culture to me.

I'd seen the occasional dysfunctional family in the streets I'd grown up in Burnley, came across people whose entire purpose in life revolved around waiting for the next giro to drop through the door and a father or two whose sole existence was to prop up the local bar and avoid the dreaded 'work' word but here I was pitched in the middle of a world where every family begged stole and borrowed. I admit those first few days were eye opening to me and the scripts certainly made me think.

I remember talking to my son Terry about it. Of course at that time *Shameless* hadn't even been screened – it would be several months before the first series hit the television schedules. I told Terry about the constant swearing and the sex scenes that seemed to happen at least once or twice a week, but he was great about it and kept telling me how proud he was of his mam.

God I hope so, I thought to myself – but just what would he make of me as a madam in a brothel? I hadn't told him that bit. As long as he didn't pester me to make an appointment with my girls I felt I could live with it. Seriously, I so wanted Terry to be proud of me and initially in the very early days I wondered where the show was going. There's a fine line between swearing for swearing's sake and sex scenes purely for shock value but it takes a good writer or two or three or four to have the sheer genius to make all of that incidental. It's in there because it's for real. I daresay the series could have been written for viewers before the watershed but then it wouldn't have had the same impact because it wouldn't have been a true depiction of sink estate life.

In time I began to realise that this was the real world and this was how a large percentage of the population lived their lives. I'd talk to David about it and wondered at first whether the writers were being a little over the top. They weren't. The show was groundbreaking and accurately portrayed real-life events on many of the so-called sink estates which exist in every city within the United Kingdom.

And so from series one we moved on to series two and then began to build up a little bit of a following. People were coming up to me in the street and asking for my autograph – or should I say for a photograph. Autographs are kind of old-fashioned these days as everybody has a mobile phone. Prior to *Shameless* I'd had the odd request for a photograph but now suddenly it was a regular occurrence. What was happening? How many people were watching this bloody show? I sensed that we were beginning to build up a bit of a cult following. (I said *cult*).

At the start of 2004, two young twins turned up on set – Elliott and Luke Tittensor who jointly played the role of Carl Gallagher. They were so cute, only about 13 years old at the time. Luke left soon after to take up a regular role in *Emmerdale* and Elliott looked a little lost without his brother so I sort of mothered him. He is such a lovely kid and I've enjoyed watching him develop into a great actor. Even now he is so very young and I think he has a tremendous career ahead of him. When he picks up his best actor Oscar in years from now I hope he mentions me because I like to think I took him under my wing a little. Be warned, Elliott!

CHAPTER 15

Awards and Recognition

Shameless was unstoppable and in early 2004 we were told we were off to the BAFTAs after the show was nominated in the Best Drama section. John Griffin got the letter and in turn he left a further letter in everyone's dressing rooms inviting us to London for the awards ceremony. *This wasn't happening*, I thought: Alice Barry, the lass from Lancashire, off to London to a swanky hotel and mixing with the stars?

The nomination was recognition for the excellent writing and, dare I say, half-decent acting too! I looked at the previous winners of the award and we were in good company. *Spooks, Buried, Cold Feet* and *Cops* were some of the past winners. I was so happy for the whole *Shameless* team but especially for the writers. As I've said before, the show was groundbreaking and took its fair share of criticism, particularly in the tabloid press; but now the British Film Academy had given us the thumbs-up. Even if we didn't win it was going to be a great evening and just being nominated was an accolade in itself.

There was a real buzz around the studio after our letters were opened. No one could quite believe it, but we all made arrangements and prepared for the big day. I remember sitting in my dressing room with Kelly Hollis discussing what we were going to wear when Kelly said we would be able to take our pick from a wardrobe department specially commissioned for the ceremony. I didn't believe her at first but she was right. We all went down on the train together and taxied to a hotel in Mayfair where we were shown to our individual rooms. I say rooms, but in actual fact they were suites and I remember the bathroom was bigger than my bathroom and my bedroom back home. We settled in and I remember enjoying the beautiful bath which was big enough for two (fancy that?) and a glass of champagne from the complimentary bottle that sat in an ice bucket by the huge window overlooking the elegant street several stories below. I was in heaven.

Soon after we were taxied to another hotel where make-up girls, hairdressers and a wardrobe crew pandered to our every need. After we had chosen our dresses we were taken through to what I can only describe as a mobile jewellery shop at the rear of the hotel. There were two huge security guards either side of the entrance and we were ushered into an Aladdin's cave of diamonds. I swear the whole room sparkled and it was clear there wasn't a fake diamond in sight. We were told to take our pick of anything we wanted and the organiser explained that we would need to sign for whatever it was we decided to wear and simply return it to them a few weeks later. There was, however, an option to purchase and obviously the retailers hoped several of the stars may just take up that option.

I opted for a beautiful diamond necklace and when the young girl placed it around my neck I knew I just had to have it. It was simply the most gorgeous thing I have ever worn and decided that I might just treat myself. I had worked hard, why not? And I didn't mind spending a couple of thousand pounds on such a beautiful piece of jewellery – after all everything else was free.

'Do you like it? the girl asked.

'Like it?' I said, 'I've positively fallen in love with it.'

I asked her how much it was.

'£62,000,' she said without a flicker of emotion.

'I'll have to think about it,' I said.

'No problem,' she said.

She handed me a business card with the company address on and I pushed it into my handbag along with the £62,000 necklace and walked out.

Several hours later we were ferried to the London Palladium in all of our finery. I remember noticing the red carpet as the taxi pulled to a stop and I wondered to myself who might I bump into.

I'd watched the BAFTAs dozens of times from the comfort of my own home and stared in wonder at the stars as they posed for photographs and signed autographs for the members of the public. Never in a hundred years would I have ever imagined that I was about to do the same. It was a surreal moment stepping onto the red carpet and as we did the flashbulbs of the photographers exploded and a burst of adrenaline surged through me. It was simply magical – one of the best moments of my life and I enjoyed every minute of it. Inside the Palladium we were welcomed with glasses of champagne and canapés and mingled with everyone else. I talked with Ant and Dec, Jimmy Nesbitt, and Andrew Lloyd Webber; I also spoke to Graham Norton who was hosting the show. Graham was an old friend, I'd been on his show and we hit it off straight away. I was at home – I felt comfortable in the company of my friends. The soap stars were all there, from *Coronation Street* and *EastEnders,* and Stephen Fry made a point of coming to talk to me. Stephen is simply gorgeous, a lovely, lovely man – it's a bit like talking to your lawyer though I don't mean that in an unkind way. He asked me if it was the first time I'd been to the BAFTAs and I said it was. He leaned into me and whispered in my ear. 'I don't think it will be the last Alice, you mark my words.'

And as you, my dear reader, are no doubt aware we won the BAFTA that year for the best drama. It was the icing on the cake. *Shameless* won a BAFTA and I was so proud to be part of that team. I was photographed that evening more times than I have been photographed in my entire life. It seemed like every press photographer in the world wanted a picture that evening and we didn't want to disappoint anyone. All too quickly the ceremony was over and we were told that we were being bussed to the Natural History Museum for an after-show party. We walked outside and down the red carpet again for more photographs and congratulations from the waiting public. I glided down the carpet that evening – it was like walking on air and I confess it took me several days to come back down to earth.

At the after-show party we got pissed (I tell it how it really is!) It was a brilliant evening and the organisers couldn't do enough for us. The champagne flowed and the music played and at one stage we even danced with our shoes off! The photographers were waiting for us again as we made our way home and I daresay there were some sorry looking states. I collapsed onto my king-sized bed in my suite back at the hotel as I rounded off a perfect day with another glass of champagne from the bottle I had opened earlier in the day. I confess the room was spinning a little but I still knew where I was (cloud nine) and couldn't quite believe the evening I had experienced. I lay back muttering to myself, 'I never thought this would be me.'

Within a few minutes I was fast asleep.

Back home in Burnley the next day I couldn't wait to tell Terry about my great adventure and show him my necklace. He nearly fell off his seat when I told him how much it cost and he wouldn't let me wear it outside of the house. I wore it a couple of times as I washed the dishes. Terry couldn't wait to get it sent back, convinced there would be a clause in the small print that would trigger payment if I kept it much longer. And although I loved it and wanted to hang on to it I knew it had to find its way back to London.

Terry was mightily relieved when I told him the necklace was on its way home. He asked me whether I had sent it registered or recorded post.

'Neither,' I said. 'I just put a few stamps on it and sent it back.'

Terry went mad. He couldn't quite believe that I'd stuffed a £62,000 necklace into a jiffy bag without any record of having sent it! He was convinced it would get lost and we would end up with the bill.

I spent a few sleepless nights, as did Terry, but a few days later I received a letter in the post from the jeweller confirming that the necklace had reached its destination.

All's well that ends well, and those wonderful memories will be with me forever.

Looking in from the outside you would have thought that everything was well with the life of Alice Barry. On the surface it was. But at home I was getting ever worried about Terry. God bless him he was 73 by now and despite what the quack of a doctor had said 36 years previously the cancer still hadn't reared its ugly head. He had however developed diabetes and now a circulation problem in his legs which was getting so bad he'd almost stopped walking anywhere. Despite his protests I insisted we went to the doctor's and he was referred to hospital. I think we both knew that something quite serious was causing the problems in Terry's legs but it was still quite a surprise when the consultant told us that he would have to undergo an operation.

On the surface Terry appeared quite happy, even though

his legs were causing him a lot of pain, and even when they weren't painful he had very little feeling in them. During the consultation Terry admitted that his legs had given way on him on several occasions – he had never mentioned this to me. The consultant explained that many of the veins in Terry's legs had simply closed and he would need to take veins or parts of veins from other parts of his body to repair the damage. The consultant was very matter of fact; it was a run of the mill type of operation, one that he carried out every few days. The consultant was very nice and we had no complaints. He said we would be notified by letter within a few weeks. I prayed that night that it would be sooner rather than later because I feared Terry was a lot worse than he was making out. Terry was never one to complain about anything but he had become very depressed. He was always an active man and being almost housebound preyed on his mind.

Sure enough within a couple of weeks the letter came. To this day I'm not sure if the operation was a success or not. Terry was allowed home almost immediately but the doctor explained one of his legs was ulcerated and would need the attention of a district nurse on a daily basis until it healed. I remember helping Terry into bed the first night I got him home. I knew his legs would be in a bit of a mess but got quite a shock when I helped him off with his shirt. They had taken most of the veins, or parts of veins from his stomach region and I took a sharp intake of breath as I first cast eyes on the patchwork quilt above and below his navel. *The poor bugger must be in agony*, I thought to myself. His legs were a hundred times worse and yet the biggest mess, the ulcerated wound, was hidden behind a large bandage. The following day the district nurse came. As I chatted with her, passing the time of day and moaning about the dismal weather, nothing could have prepared me from what she was about to reveal behind the blood-soaked dressings. It was simply awful, like raw red meat, and it looked like what I can only describe as a big dirty hole. *My God*, I thought, *how on earth have they allowed him out of hospital?*

At first it didn't seem to bother Terry, while the nurse took it all in her stride telling me she had seen a lot worse. She came in every day for three or four weeks and began to get a little concerned that the wound wasn't showing any sign of healing or indeed closing up. Terry's body was not doing its job and he slipped ever deeper into depression, frustrated that despite the operation he still couldn't take more than a few steps and walking to the local shops or the pub was simply a bridge too far.

But he did try. He was determined to push himself as far as he could and I caught him several times lying on the floor as he'd collapsed trying to get to the bathroom or the kitchen unaided. And believe me at six foot four and 15 stone he made quite a noise when he hit the floor. The trouble was I couldn't get him up once he was down there and he just didn't have the strength in his legs to help himself. Luckily my son Terry didn't live far away and most of the times my husband collapsed, my son Terry would run over as fast as he could. Between the two of us we could just about manage to get him up and into bed. It took an awful lot out of him and each time it happened I knew it hit him hard and his will to win through gradually dissolved before my very eyes. I think looking back on it now Terry was upset because he felt he was losing his dignity. He was a giant of a man and always busy and active and very independent. Now here he was relying on others and it tore him apart. On one occasion he collapsed and I couldn't get hold of Terry Junior so I had to phone an ambulance. Terry pleaded with me not to call them but I had no option: I couldn't bear to see him floundering on the bedroom floor. Here was the biggest, strongest man in the world – my rock – broken and as helpless as a day-old kitten. But Terry wouldn't give up trying to get around and he started collapsing on a regular basis. They told me he would need to come into hospital again and to be honest it was the best place for him because I was simply unable to cope with his sheer size. Having said that, Terry was beginning to lose weight. He wasn't fat, he was never fat, but I believed the fact he'd lost a couple of stone wouldn't do him any harm. When he was in hospital there was someone there to help him 24 hours a day and of course they kept him in bed and stopped him from trying to walk around. I think part of him gave up then. He lost the will to live and kind of realised that this was the end, although at the time I didn't think that. But Terry was apart from his beloved family in a sterile, alien environment. He couldn't walk anywhere and he started to waste away before my very eyes. I wanted to bring him home but everybody told me he was in the best place, which I understood completely.

He'd been in hospital about two weeks and I was preparing for my daily visit when the telephone rang. The hospital told me I needed to get there urgently as his system was beginning to close down. I rang my son Terry and we rushed over as quickly as we could. The hospital priest was waiting for us when we got there to administer the last rites and although it was a bit of a shock it was not altogether unexpected. My poor husband couldn't even speak to us. He wanted to but it was beyond his capabilities. We stayed with him until the early hours of the morning and about three o'clock my son Terry and I decided to go to the chapel in the hospital to pray. We'd been there about an hour when a nurse came to fetch us. She didn't tell us what was wrong, just asked us to pop along and be with him. But her eyes told me that death was closing in on him. She was right. Terry died within 30 minutes as I held one hand and my son held the other.

It was the end of the world for me, it really was. He had been by my side for 44 years and I thought I would be unable to cope. How do you go on when part of your life is taken from you like that? And of course the experience brought back my parents' deaths and my brother Tommy's death too, and all I wanted to do was curl up in a ball and go to sleep forever.

But you don't, do you? You realise that life has to go on and your friends and family rally round. It was then I realised how many friends I had and how important they were to me. I had only been working with the *Shameless* cast and crew for just over two years but it was as if they had been my friends for a lifetime. Lawrence Till, the director of *Shameless*, was one of the first to come and visit, as was Kelly

Hollis, and the bouquets of flowers and cards came by the van-load. I read every one and they meant so much to me and I still have them to this day. I don't have the flowers, of course, but the cards I kept and every now and again when I'm feeling a little bit tearful or a little sentimental I pull them out and have a read and a few tears to myself. It reminds me how lucky I am in life to have such wonderful friends and I try to remember Terry before his illness incapacitated him.

I took two weeks off work and tried to rally myself round. It was difficult at first but then again as soon as I stepped into the studio it was as if I'd never been away. Everyone was so kind and so welcoming and my dressing room was full of more flowers and a dozen more cards and as I read them I had a few more tears. Jeff Hewitt, the transport manager who I'd known for over five years, was especially good and always knocked on my dressing room door when he passed to offer a reassuring word or two and a cuddle if I needed it. Occasionally he'd wander in with two cups of tea and sit down and we'd natter like two old women.

I got through it with a lot of help from my friends and I coped because I told myself I'd had 44 wonderful years with the best husband in the world. How many people can say that?

And life continued. My wonderful life and my wonderful job continued, albeit without the man I loved. My working day at the studio carried on as normal and I began to laugh and joke again with the characters who had laughed and joked with me all along. David still wound me up and took the piss out of me; I wouldn't have had it any other way and he helped me more than he could ever imagine.

Shameless went from strength to strength, the viewing figures increased series after series and it was sold to Australia, Belgium, New Zealand, Canada, France, Holland, Finland, Portugal, Ireland, Israel, Latin America and, of course, the United States of America where the remake show has become such a big hit. At first I didn't think I would like that, Frank Gallagher as an American, but I have to say I've watched it and it works.

It's a true saying, 'time is a great healer', and slowly but surely I began to get my life back.

CHAPTER 16

The Odd Couple

I had always known Jeff Hewitt on and around the
Shameless studio set and recalled he'd worked on other
productions I had been involved with in the past. Fate,
however, appeared to be pulling us closer and closer
together. It was now over a year since Terry had died and I
started to develop a confusing attraction towards Jeff. I was
beginning to enjoy his company more and more and when
Jeff wasn't around for a day or two I started to miss him. We
started going out together, not on dates I hasten to add, just
nights out at the pub or for an occasional meal. As the
relationship developed we grew more and more comfortable
in each other's company and although I can never describe
him as a replacement for Terry he did seem to fill a void. I
felt like I'd climbed another small hurdle in getting over

Terry and for the first time I was enjoying male company again. It was clear we were becoming fonder of each other and yet at that point I would describe it as more of a brother and sister type relationship.

And then one day Jeff really confused me, he suggested we take a week's holiday in Andalucía, in Spain at his friend's villa in a town called Mijas. Jeff said I needed a break and it was true I hadn't had a holiday since Terry died, not even a weekend away. The week's holiday really appealed to me and the weather at the time in England was dreary and dull. I knew it made sense and I Googled Mijas to find out a little bit more about it. It looked idyllic and then one day Jeff brought in some photographs of his friend's villa. It was simply gorgeous and I had to go. I told Jeff there and then that I was up for it. As the time to fly out to Spain approached I began to feel more than a little uncomfortable and yet part of me so wanted to go. I was having second thoughts and wondered what Terry would say if he was looking down on me from above going on holiday with another man.

I had two little gremlins on my shoulders. One said 'Don't be silly, go and have a good time' and the other was shouting 'Jezebel'. I never thought for one minute that something more would develop and yet I couldn't help wondering that we were being pitched into an environment where it was possible and I just didn't want to take that chance.

And then the solution came to me. I would take my sister-in-law Pam with me. Although Pam was my sister-in-law she was also one of my best friends and always up for a good time and a laugh and joke. I knew she would agree to go and sure enough she jumped at the chance of a week in the sun and before I came off the phone I could almost hear her starting to pack her case.

Poor Jeff.

I couldn't quite gauge his reaction when I asked if Pam could come. I don't know if part of him was offended but if he was he didn't show it. He was just Jeff. Dear old sweet Jeff and he said it would be fine and that we'd all have a great time together.

And we did. It was a magical week: lovely and warm and the sun shone from dawn till dusk as we sat out on the terrace until the early hours of the morning drinking ice cold Spanish Cava, swapping jokes and telling stories from our past. It was during that week that I really bonded with Jeff, we shared secrets with each other and we had a few tears too as I told him everything that Terry meant to me. The relationship took on a new meaning. During that week we became soul mates. Poor Pam. Oh dear, I'm sorry Pam if you felt your nose was pushed out that week, but me and Jeff really hit it off.

We arrived back to a wet and windy Manchester airport. Nothing changes. I began staying over at Jeff's house in Manchester on Friday evenings and staying the weekend. It seemed pointless going back to an empty house in Burnley.

We were regular revellers at the top Manchester nightspots that Jeff knew so well. It was like having your own guide to lead you by the hand.

Some time later we decided on a weekend in Blackpool.

My good friend Bobby Ball had mentioned the Queens Hotel in the town run by Pat Mancini (known locally as the Queen of Blackpool) and said it was the number one place to go, often frequented by the local showbiz set, including Joe Longthorne, Chubby Brown and Frank Carson who I also knew. It seemed the ideal place to be, so I looked up the number and telephoned the hotel. I rang from my dressing room while Jeff was there. The receptionist asked me how many people would be staying and I gave her the names. 'Will that be a double room or a twin?' she asked in all innocence.

Jeff was listening in on the conversation and as I said two single rooms please he told me not to be silly.

'Just get a twin room,' he whispered. 'It will be cheaper.'

That's Jeff, ever the accountant and businessman. And so we did. We booked a twin room.

I was mortified as we stood in the reception area of the Queens Hotel in Blackpool. Me, a married woman – albeit widowed – sharing a room with a single man! I really wish there had been a confession box somewhere in that hotel because if there had been I would've jumped into it and confessed everything. I was convinced that every set of eyes in the hotel were staring at me.

Later that evening we met Pat Mancini. It was the beginning of a wonderful friendship that would last up until her untimely death in 2011. She was 72, a year younger than my husband Terry when God took him. I took great comfort from Pat's niece Victoria at her funeral service when she said 'Auntie was an Angel and it proves God only takes the very best.' It was such a nice thing to say. Pat made us very welcome that first evening we met her and such was her warmth and vibrancy we were drawn like a magnet time and time again back to her beautiful hotel.

At the end of that first evening, Jeff and I retired to our twin room and we both slept like babies. Sharing a room with him was such a natural thing to do.

People looking in from the outside could be forgiven for thinking there is more to our relationship. They have described us as inseparable and its true we hold hands often and hug and kiss each other (not wet tonguey ones of course!) and yes we are very touchy-feely with each other. We are both as mad as each other and there's never a dull moment in our company with Jeff always ready to crack a joke or clown around. If I were to be asked to describe our relationship in one word that would be easy: I would say fun.

It works. Our relationship works and is very special to us. We are like brother and sister, husband and wife, best friends and above all soul mates too. Soul mates are how I like to describe our relationship with people when they are bold enough to ask.

If you are trying to work Alice and Jeff out then I would say don't. You'll probably never get there. We are ecstatically happy as we are and have no plans to change things. There is, after all, an old saying that states if the roof isn't broken don't fix it.

CHAPTER 17

Life Today

I am fortunate that the career path I chose (or rather that chose me) gave me the type of financial stability I could only dream of and I try to give a little back to those less fortunate than myself. Pat Mancini was a great 'charity' girl, always ready to organise and contribute to literally dozens of worthy causes. If I can achieve a fraction of what Pat achieved then I'll die happy and hopefully go to the right place in later life.

And for that reason I think whenever the organisers of charity auction events are compiling a guest list the name 'Alice Barry' surely has to be top of the guest list. I confess I'm an absolute sucker for those sorts of parties and occasionally I get a little carried away. It's a heady mixture, usually a nice dinner then a little alcohol and the feeling that you are doing your bit. I make no apologies, I feel good when I help charities and whenever possible I do my utmost to attend. The lounge and dining room at Barry's Hotel is full of memorabilia that I've collected over the years by bidding successfully, (usually for silly money) on photographs, football shirts, signed prints.

I love them and even when I have paid way over the odds for something I get an enormous amount of pleasure as my gaze falls on them almost daily. And of course I relay each story to the guests who come to stay at Barry's hotel as they enquire how they have come into my possession and I take even more pleasure in their pleasure which is clear to see. I can honestly say I have no regrets buying anything but dread to think of the many thousands of pounds I have spent over the years.

I recall being at one auction and bidding over £3,000 for a David Beckham signed shirt complete with frame. I follow Manchester United (and Blackpool too) and simply adore David Beckham and I had to have it. When the bidding topped the £3,000 mark my throat was dry and I had sobered up rapidly. £3,200, £3,300 – the bids were going higher and higher jumping a £100 at a time.

Jeff was with me at the time and I remember he took hold of my arm and said 'You sure you want to pay this much?' I shrugged my shoulders, 'I'm not sure,' I said. 'We are getting into realms of silly money'. No sooner had I answered Jeff than the hammer came down on the gavel and the auctioneer said 'Sold!'

I looked around to see who the lucky recipient was at the auctioneer was pointing to me.

'Sold to Alice Barry,' he said. 'Sold for £3,600.'

I was absolutely ecstatic and couldn't wait to rush over to give the organisers my details and take delivery of the magnificent frame to take pride of place in the dining room of Barry's Hotel.

As I was signing my name a businessman rushed over to me offering me £4,000 for the shirt. He said he had been trying to bid but had been at the back of the room and the auctioneer had missed his hand in the darkness. I felt sorry for him as he clearly wanted the shirt and said something about his son's birthday. I almost gave in but then thought about how much I loved Beckham myself. I also knew how much pleasure it would give the guests at Barry's and more people would see it hanging on my dining room wall than a rich businessman's son's bedroom.

I politely declined his offer.

However something else was catching my ear. The auctioneer was in full flow again as I provided the organisers with my credit card details. I heard 'meet and greet' and I heard 'Manchester'. Did I also detect the word 'United'? This was fantastic – it was some sort of event for two people, probably a football match where I would be able to meet and greet the Manchester United players. I didn't care whether there was a football match or not, it was incidental, I would be able to meet my heroes. Seeing them play would be an added bonus. I simply had to have it.

The bidding reached £500 and I joined in.

£550…£600…£650.

'£700!' I called out as I threw my arm in the air.

The auctioneer grinned, 'It's Alice Barry again!' he cried out. A few people around me gave me a round of applause and the hammer came down yet again in my favour.

I'd done it! What a great night it was turning out to be, if a little expensive.

I turned to the girl who was still holding my credit card and told her to add an extra £700 on. She leaned over and gave me a kiss on the cheek and thanked me for being so generous to the charity. Her kind words meant an awful lot to me.

She pointed me towards an open door at the back of the room. 'You can collect your things in there at the end,' she said.

There were a few more things up for auction but soon the night was over and I couldn't wait to collect the two items I'd won. There were dozens of people in the room but I waited patiently until eventually I had my hands on that shirt and what I thought were tickets for the Manchester United game and a meet and greet the players afterwards.

'Here are your Madness tickets,' the girl said.

'What?'

'Your Madness tickets, they are in concert and you can go backstage and meet them.'

Suddenly it dawned on me that this wasn't a meet and greet of Manchester United players, it was a meet and greet Madness concert... IN MANCHESTER!

I'd misheard. Bugger bugger bugger!

However, I wasn't about to renege on my bid and ask for my money back. It was all for charity, after all, and I would puff out my chest, accept my little mistake and get on with it.

I thought to myself it would be nice to see Madness in concert and to have a drink with the lads afterwards. They'd seemed like nice chaps when I'd watched them on TV.

We got the tickets transferred to Blackpool as Madness were appearing there too. After the concert the organisers had put on a small buffet and some drinks in the bar at the back of the theatre. Jeff and I stood with a group of fans who had paid extra to meet their heroes. Some had won competitions in newspapers and magazines. The atmosphere was fantastic as everybody anticipated the arrival of the band.

They never arrived; we waited around for more than an hour but they never showed. A rather embarrassed lady walked into the bar and apologised profusely but said the band weren't coming; instead they were on their way to Edinburgh for the Fringe.

I'm not going to turn around and say that I didn't like the Madness concert as I did, I enjoyed it immensely – especially the warm up act, The Beautiful South. But I wasn't impressed when they didn't turn up to the party.

Personally I wasn't too bothered one way or the other about actually meeting them, but people had paid good money to attend that party. They must have known that all those fans were dying to see them and that it was a once-in-a-lifetime opportunity for some of them.

The fans were absolutely stunned and it was an awkward and embarrassing moment for the poor girl who had to try to explain what had happened. One poor lad was in tears. Jeff and I left our drinks and walked out.

CHAPTER 18

The Future

The final chapter of my book, my biographer tells me, has to be about my take on life. At this point I must give a little pat on the back to Ken Scott who has helped me on this quite remarkable journey. He calls himself a biographer, although his website mentions the word 'ghostwriter' quite a few times and I confess I was a little confused when I first saw the term. His explanation, however, cleared the muddy waters quite rapidly. He told me he will ghostwrite a book for someone who can't write. For example I have read his highly-acclaimed account of Horace Greasley, an incredible man who escaped from Prisoner of War camps in Poland over 200 times to meet up with a German girl and bring much-needed food into the camp from the surrounding villages. Scotty met Horace when he was 90 years of age and the dear old man couldn't even hold a pen, let alone manage to boot up a modern computer. Arthritis had claimed his fingers many years ago.

'With you, Alice, and the likes of Crissy Rock,' (he was her biographer on her bestselling autobiography *This Heart Within Me Burns*) 'it's a little different because I know you can write. You just need a good foot up the arse, a focus and a direction and your words tweaked a little.'

I fear he was being a little modest because he also acted as a teacher of sorts and showed me how to construct a chapter, building it into a sort of mini book on its own with a beginning, middle and an end, and leaving the reader on the edge of a precipice wanting more with no option but to turn the pages quickly to find out what happens. It was tough at first but gradually it all started to come together and fit into place.

Anyway, I digress. Scotty insisted that I was very opinionated on a whole host of topics and said that it would have more of an impact if I voiced some of them towards the end of the book. It would give the reader a greater insight into the sort of person I was. I didn't think I had opinions but as Scotty analysed some of the subjects we'd covered over the last six months I began to realize that perhaps he was right.

I'd never really thought too deeply about the type of characters and estates on *Shameless*, for example, but as he went over our notes and interview recordings he brought up a whole host of things that at first I thought had come from the lips of William Hague or David Cameron. They hadn't; they were my notes and my voice on the tapes and some of them took me by surprise.

Shameless estates. They are out there you'd better believe it. Some people ask me for my opinions and solutions in eradicating the problems that exist within these communities. I haven't got the answer I'm afraid and the truth is that there are sometimes three or four generations within a family who have known nothing but life on the dole and handouts from the government.

There will always be people who are happy to live that way to breeze through life merely existing and not achieving anything of any substance. I feel sad for them, I really do, but I say live and let live. I'm in my 60s now and possibly won't be around in another 20 years. But even now, if the good Lord was to decide my number was up I look back on my life with pride in what I have achieved and the people I have worked with. The list is endless and I've met some incredible characters, been to television awards ceremonies and treated like a VIP. My life is very special and I never take anything for granted.

I happily pose with people for photographs and give them autographs as I know I am in a very privileged position. But I have also worked to achieve that status and made many sacrifices along the way.

I remember as a little girl in Burnley, there was a man who lived just a few doors away from us. Old Mr Williams was on benefits for as long as I could remember and even boasted that he had a handout from the government to buy dog food for his little dog. He never worked a day in his life and was never out of the pub. He lay in bed every day until half an hour before the pubs opened at 11 o'clock. He made himself a cup of tea and a little breakfast and walked the short distance to the pub at the end of the road just in time for the doors opening.

He drank beer and played dominoes until the pub closed, went home to sleep it off and was back again for the evening session. For those of you from the younger generation that was the pub licensing law at the time. A pub opened at 11am and closed at 3pm, normally opening up again at around 6pm again for the evening shift.

I remember my father being quite animated about Mr Williams, telling my mother that his benefits should be stopped. He looked old but was a long way off retirement age and my dad swore he had at least 10 years work left in him. But of course he never did. He played the system and I suppose he thought himself quite clever. But he never saw anything of the world – he never looked any further than his own front street and the pub at the end of the road. His house was full of old second-hand furniture and I can't ever recall him in a new shirt or a pair of trousers. His clothes were threadbare, his shoes full of holes and he couldn't even spell the word 'holiday'. He was sad, but then again I'm guessing he was happy in his own little world he had created for himself. Live and let live that's what I say, if that's the way people want to live their lives then let them get on with it.

However I do think that there are two distinct people on benefits. There are those that want to work and can't, and those that don't want to work at all. I think it would be quite easy to suss out the latter group and I think that they should be counselled by certain individuals with a passion for life and made to see the error of their ways. The world is a wonderful place, life is good and can be very rewarding if you choose to get out there and achieve something. But in order to do that you must make an effort to get out of bed in the morning. You need to set goals and targets and what better by way of reward is to buy something you really wanted or take a trip to a country you've always wanted to visit?

And at the very least these individuals should be made to serve the community in which they live in or end up having their benefits cut. It annoys me so much for example when we get a bad cold spell like we did last year and see snow lying on the paths in our towns and villages and cities. There are old people who were unable to take a walk to the shops last year for four or five weeks because of the snow and ice that seemed to stay around forever. It's wrong and I can't believe that anyone fit enough can't be handed a shovel and set to work. Surely it can't be that difficult?

As I said some people are happy with their lot in life and if that's the way they want to be so be it. We are all different characters and some have ambition more than most. I can relate to my school friends who spent a lifetime in the factories and mills of Burnley and I daresay most of them have enjoyed life and are as happy as the next person. An actress's life is the life everyone would want to choose. Even now at the ripe old age of 67 I can leave the house at seven in the morning and not return until after 10 or 11 at night. Most women my age are retired and have their feet up but it's not something I've ever thought about. I daresay I'll continue until the day *Shameless* dispenses with Lillian's services or until I drop dead onset. I love acting and I love what acting has given to me over the years. I'm always grateful to my employers for giving me the opportunity to travel. I've been to Australia, Singapore, Las Vegas and Cyprus and most places in Europe. I've never had to think about saving money to go places as I've been permanently employed for the last 20 years. I know without acting I would never have been able to visit the countries I have visited but I feel I've earned it and I feel I've deserved it. I've already touched on the many awards ceremonies I've attended and I've lost count as to the number of four and five-star hotels I've stayed in as a result and yes, sometimes I look back and think who would have thought that. A Burnley lass that's me, a poorly educated, unqualified, working class Burnley lass who started out life in a factory and look what's happened to me as the years have gone by.

So what next? The truth is I don't know. I can't think there is anything left in life I really want to achieve. I don't want to stop acting and would probably die a happy lady if I dropped down many years from now on the set of *Shameless* though I daresay it would give everyone else a little shock. I hope the series runs and runs and I sincerely believe it will because it's that good.

At the time of writing, Jeff and I are handing over the reins of Barry's Hotel to someone else and may try another business adventure (watch this space) somewhere else. Don't worry I'm sure you will certainly hear about it when we do.

Thank you, my dear, reader for sharing this special journey

with me and I hope you have enjoyed the experience as much as I did. If you have ever had any inclination to write a book then I would say try it. It's surprising what you can achieve if you put your mind to something. Remember, life is like a lemon, you've got to squeeze it as hard as you can.

If it's meant to happen then it will; whatever's meant for you won't pass you by.